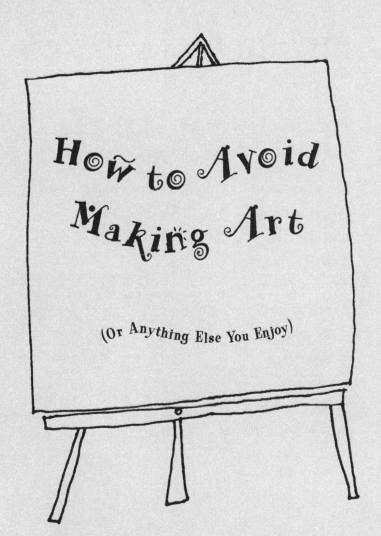

How to Avoid Making Art

Making Art

(Or Anything Else You Enjoy)

Also by Julia Cameron

NONFICTION

The Artist's Way

Walking in This World

The Vein of Gold

The Right to Write

The Sound of Paper

Answered Prayers

Heart Steps

Blessings

Transitions

Prayers from a Nonbeliever

Letters to a Young Artist

The Artist's Way Morning
Pages Journal

The Artist's Date Book
(illustrated by Elizabeth Cameron)

Supplies

God Is No Laughing Matter

God Is Dog Spelled Backwards
(illustrated by Elizabeth Cameron)

Inspirations: Meditations from
The Artist's Way

The Writer's Life: Insights from
The Right to Write

The Artist's Way at Work
(with Mark Bryan and Catherine Allen)

Money Drunk, Money Sober
(with Mark Bryan)

FICTION

Popcorn: Hollywood Stories

The Dark Room

PLAYS

Public Lives

The Animal in the Trees

Four Roses

Love in the DMZ

Avalon (a musical)

The Medium at Large (a musical)

POETRY

Prayers for the Little Ones

Prayers to the Nature Spirits

The Quiet Animal

This Earth
(also an album with Tim Wheater)

FEATURE FILM
(as writer-director)

God's Will

Illustrations by
Elizabeth Cameron

Jeremy P. Tarcher/Penguin
a member of Penguin Group (USA) Inc.
New York

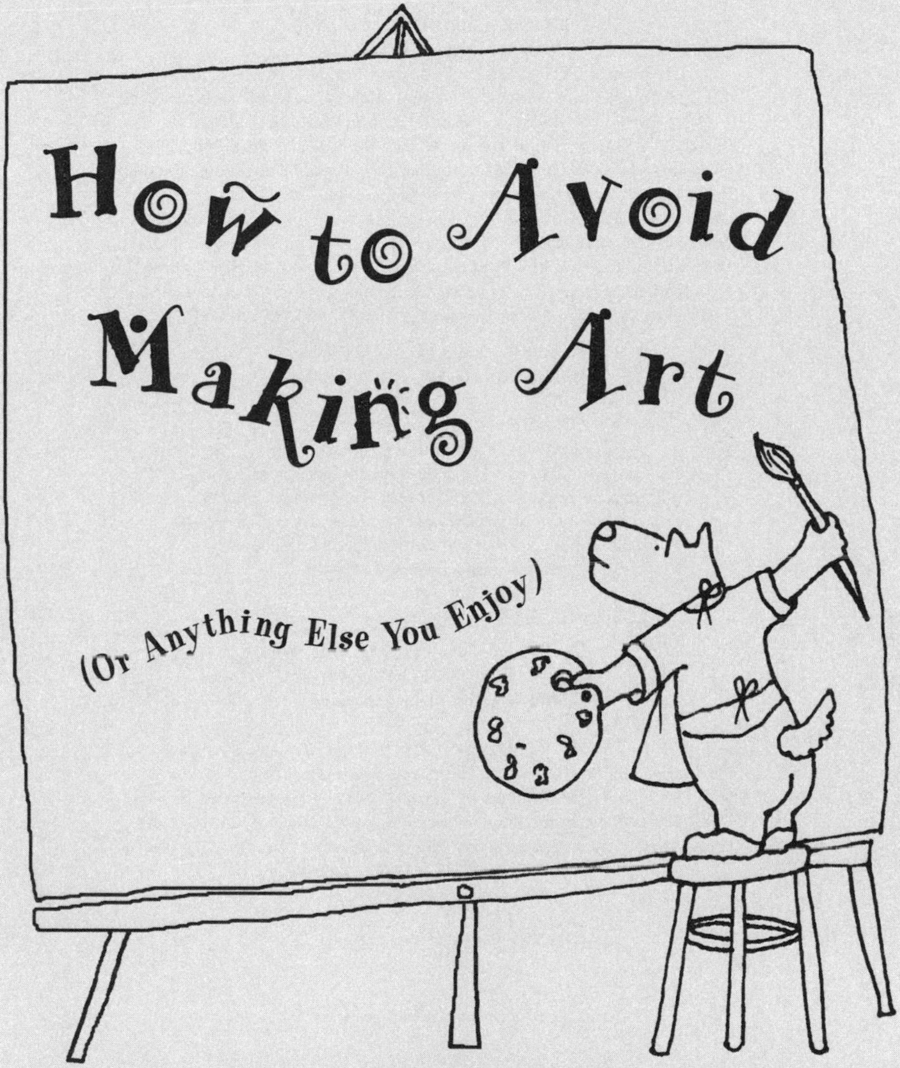
How to Avoid Making Art
(Or Anything Else You Enjoy)

Julia Cameron

JEREMY P. TARCHER/PENGUIN
Published by the Penguin Group
Penguin Group (USA) Inc., 375 Hudson Street, New York, New York 10014,
USA • Penguin Group (Canada), 90 Eglinton Avenue East, Suite 700, Toronto,
Ontario M4P 2Y3, Canada (a division of Pearson Penguin Canada Inc.) •
Penguin Books Ltd, 80 Strand, London WC2R 0RL, England • Penguin Ireland,
25 St Stephen's Green, Dublin 2, Ireland (a division of Penguin Books Ltd) • Penguin
Group (Australia), 250 Camberwell Road, Camberwell, Victoria 3124, Australia
(a division of Pearson Australia Group Pty Ltd) • Penguin Books India Pvt Ltd, 11
Community Centre, Panchsheel Park, New Delhi–110 017, India • Penguin Group
(NZ), Cnr Airborne and Rosedale Roads, Albany, Auckland 1310, New Zealand
(a division of Pearson New Zealand Ltd) • Penguin Books (South Africa)
(Pty) Ltd, 24 Sturdee Avenue, Rosebank, Johannesburg 2196, South Africa

Penguin Books Ltd, Registered Offices:
80 Strand, London WC2R 0RL, England

Library of Congress Cataloging-in-Publication Data

Cameron, Julia.
How to avoid making art (or anything else you enjoy) / Julia Cameron ;
illustrations by Elizabeth Cameron.
p.   cm.
ISBN 1-58542-438-2
1. Creative ability—Humor.   2. Creation (Literary, artistic, etc.)—Humor.
3. Self-defeating behavior—Humor.   4. Creative ability—Caricatures and cartoons.
5. Creation (Literary, artistic, etc.)—Caricatures and cartoons.   6. Self-defeating
behavior—Caricatures and cartoons.   I. Evans, Elizabeth Cameron.   II. Title.
BF411.C357   2005   2005046484
153.3'5—dc22

Printed in the United States of America
1   3   5   7   9   10   8   6   4   2

This book is printed on acid-free paper. ∞

Book design by Meighan Cavanaugh

Most Tarcher/Penguin books are available at special quantity discounts for bulk
purchase for sales promotions, premiums, fund-raising, and educational needs. Special
books or book excerpts also can be created to fit specific needs. For details, write
Penguin Group (USA) Inc. Special Markets, 375 Hudson Street, New York, NY 10014.

This book is dedicated to

the wit and humor

of our parents,

Jim and Dorothy Cameron

Acknowledgments

John Bodeau, for his character and company

The Cameron Siblings, for their wit

Sara Carder, for her fine stewardship

Sonia Choquette, for her levity and her gravity

Rhonda Flemming, for her whimsy

Gerard Hackett, for his one-liners

Bernice Hill, for her clear-eyed view

Jack Hofsiss, for his comedy

Elberta Honstein, for her optimistic strength

Joel Fotinos, for his laughter and leadership

Emma Lively, for her liveliness

Larry Lonergan, for his twinkling spirit

Fran Martin, for her independent outlook

Julianna McCarthy, for her droll good humor

Bob McDonald, for his robust laugh

Bruce Pomahac, for his comedic spark

Domenica Cameron-Scorsese, for her resilience in the trenches

Dr. Robert Smith, for his grounded priorities

Jeremy Tarcher, for his insights

Edmund Towle, for his sly wit

Bill Wilson, for his visionary ideals

Elizabeth Winick, for her grace

How to Avoid Making Art
(Or Anything Else You Enjoy)

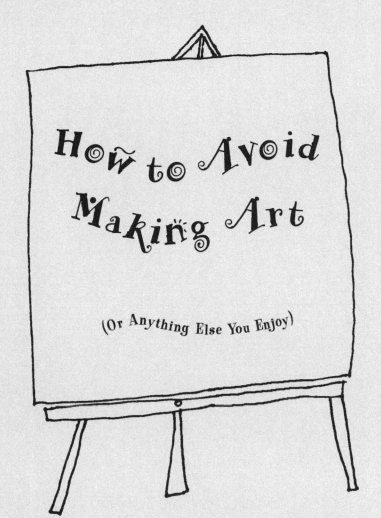

HOW TO AVOID
MAKING ART?
MAKE YOUR
FIRST PROJECT
REALLY BIG.

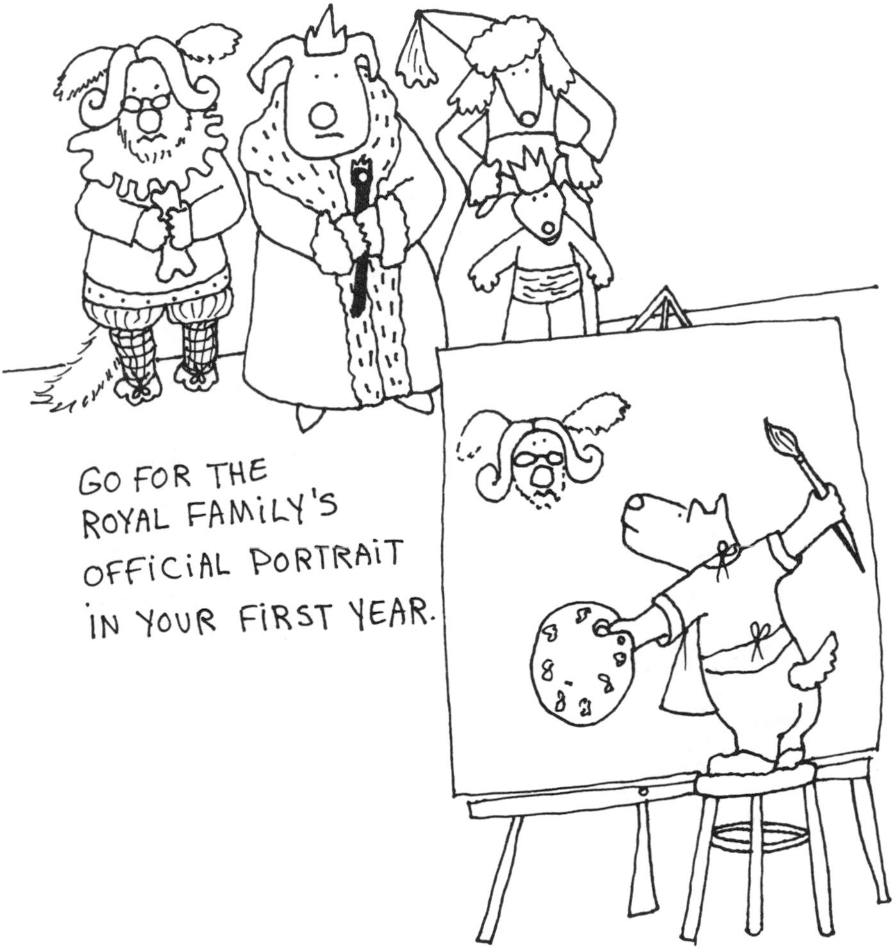

GO FOR THE ROYAL FAMILY'S OFFICIAL PORTRAIT IN YOUR FIRST YEAR.

SIGN ON WITH A THERAPIST WHO
CONSIDERS THE CREATIVE PROCESS
MYSTERIOUS AND DANGEROUS. LOOK FOR ONE WHO
USES WORDS LIKE "COMPENSATION." SPEND YOUR
SESSIONS AND YOUR MONEY DISCUSSING WHY YOU
CAN'T CREATE INSTEAD OF HOW YOU COULD.

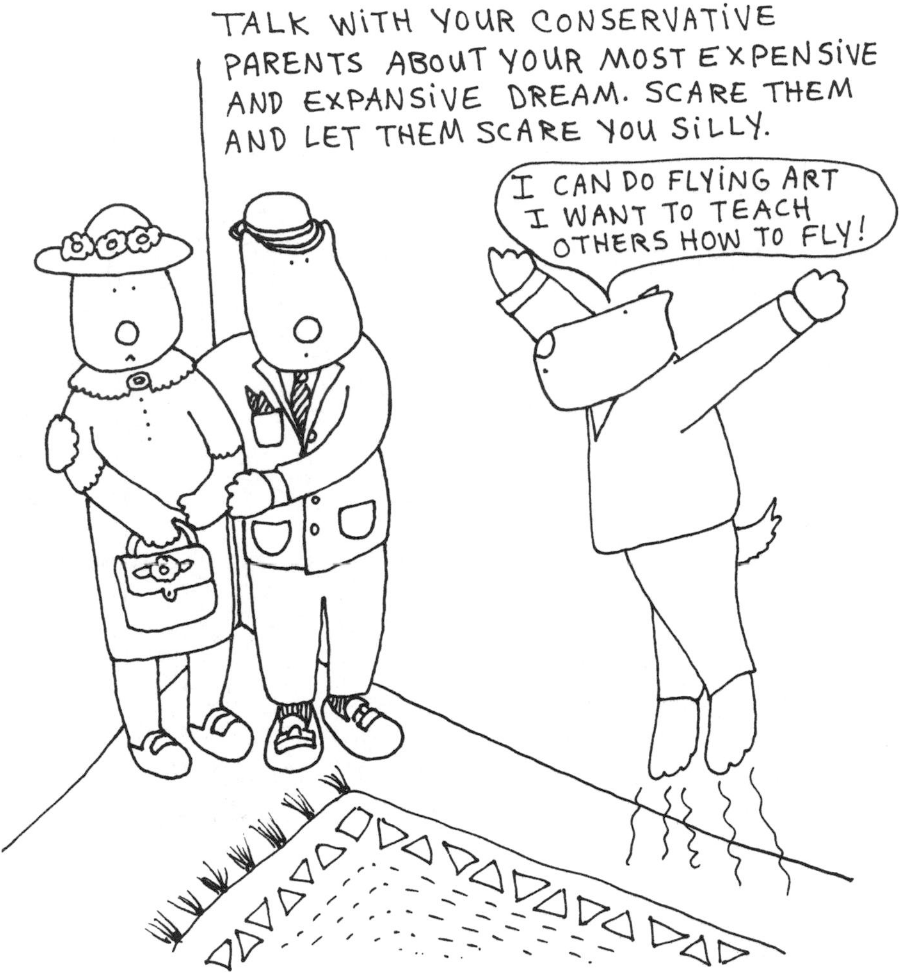

TALK WITH YOUR CONSERVATIVE PARENTS ABOUT YOUR MOST EXPENSIVE AND EXPANSIVE DREAM. SCARE THEM AND LET THEM SCARE YOU SILLY.
I CAN DO FLYING ART I WANT TO TEACH OTHERS HOW TO FLY!

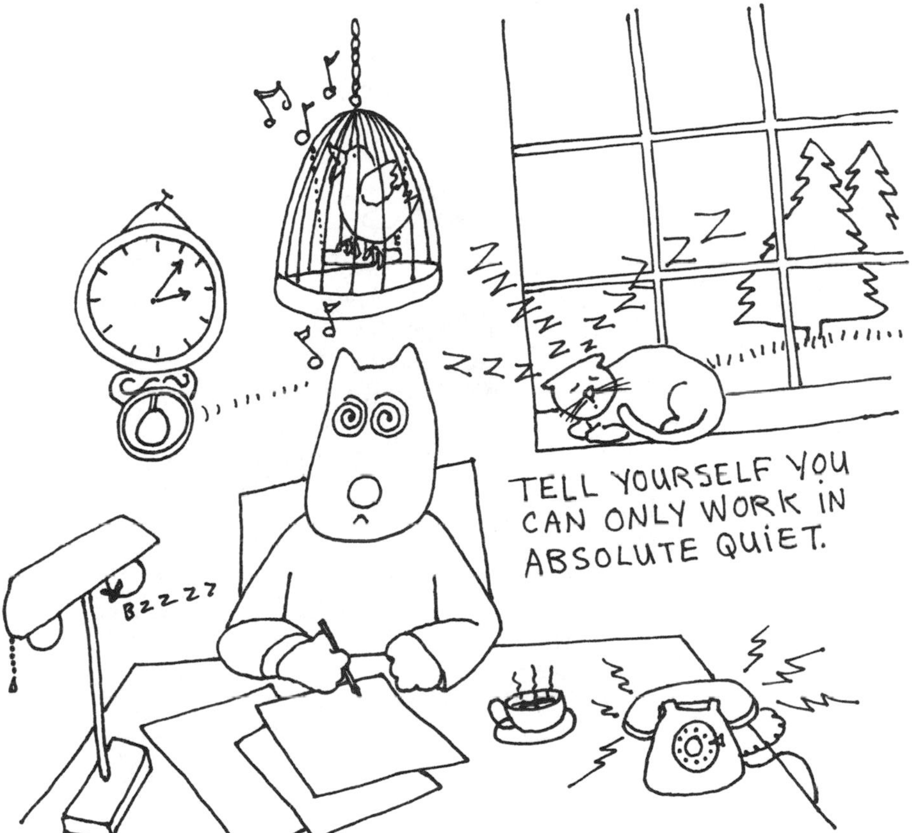
TELL YOURSELF YOU
CAN ONLY WORK IN
ABSOLUTE QUIET.

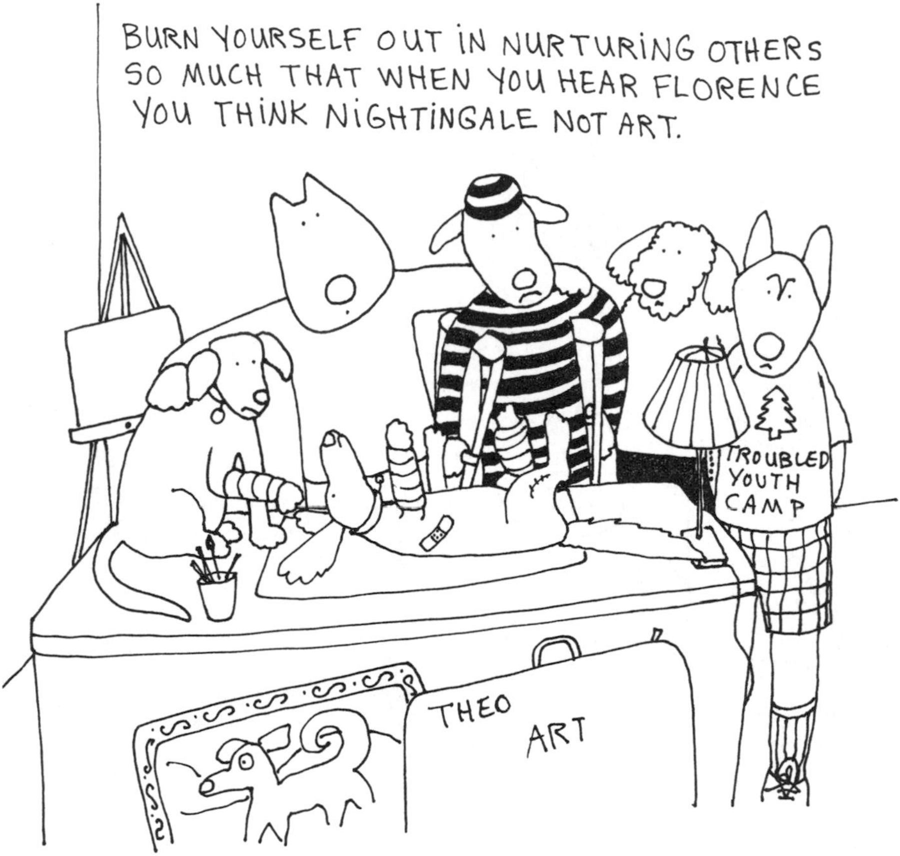
BURN YOURSELF OUT IN NURTURING OTHERS SO MUCH THAT WHEN YOU HEAR FLORENCE YOU THINK NIGHTINGALE NOT ART.
TROUBLED YOUTH CAMP
THEO
ART

COMPARE YOUR
WORK TO THE
MASTERWORKS
OF THE GREAT
MASTERS.

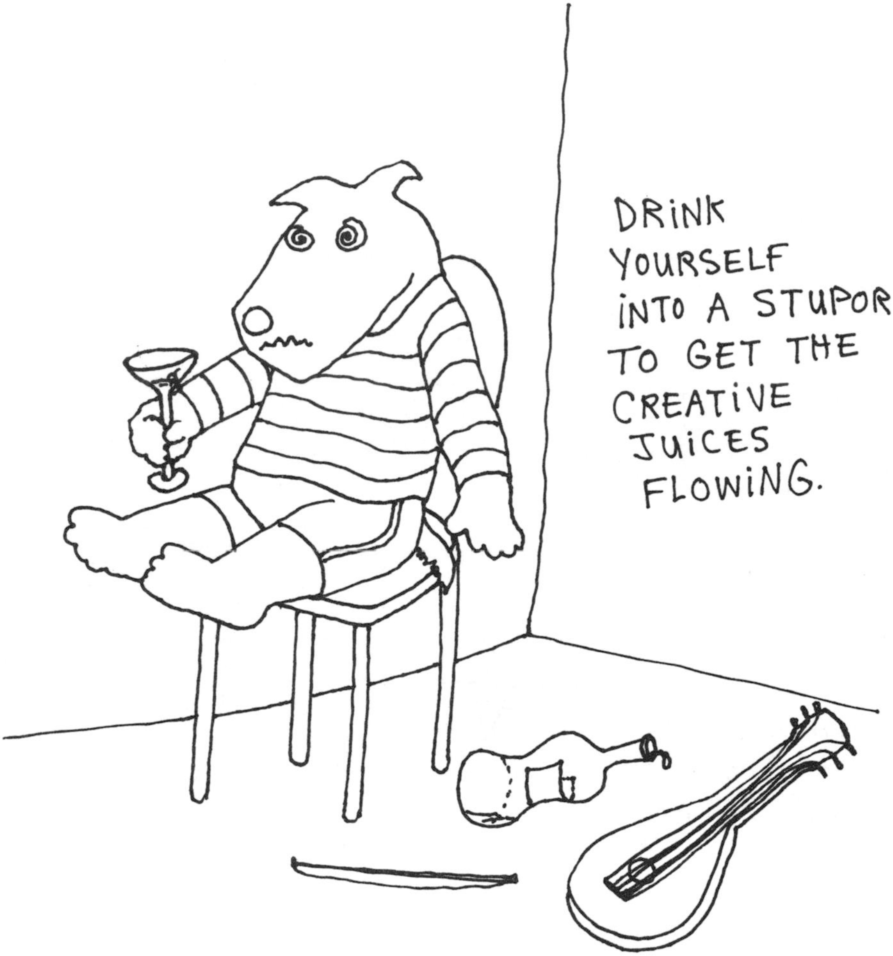
DRINK
YOURSELF
INTO A STUPOR
TO GET THE
CREATIVE
JUICES
FLOWING.

SMOKE A LOT OF DOPE FOR INSPIRATION.
FORGET WHY IT'S CALLED DOPE.
FORGET YOUR INSPIRATIONS.

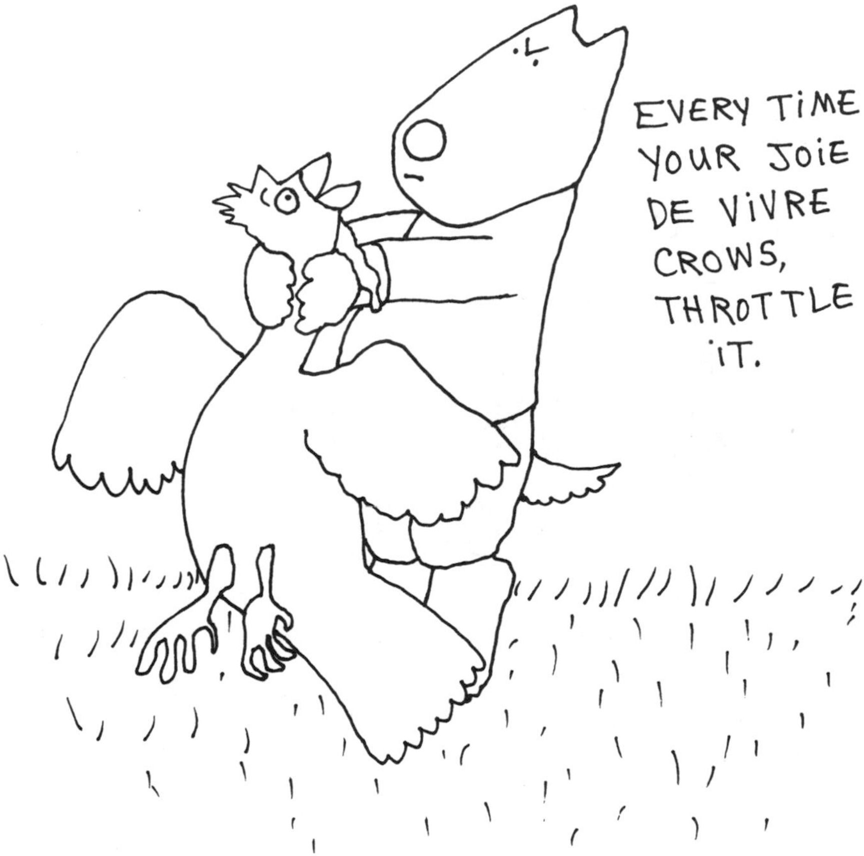
EVERY TIME YOUR JOIE DE VIVRE CROWS, THROTTLE IT.

ATTEMPT SOMETHING REALLY COMPLICATED.

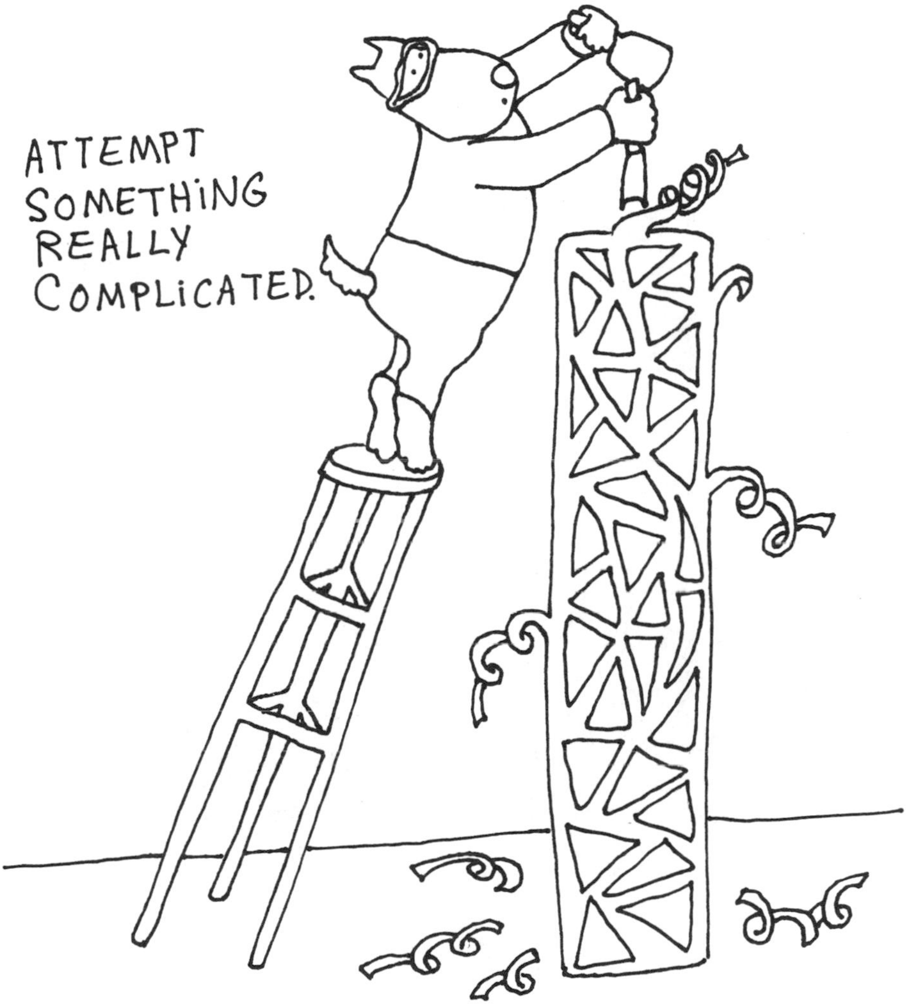

BE IN A BIG HURRY.

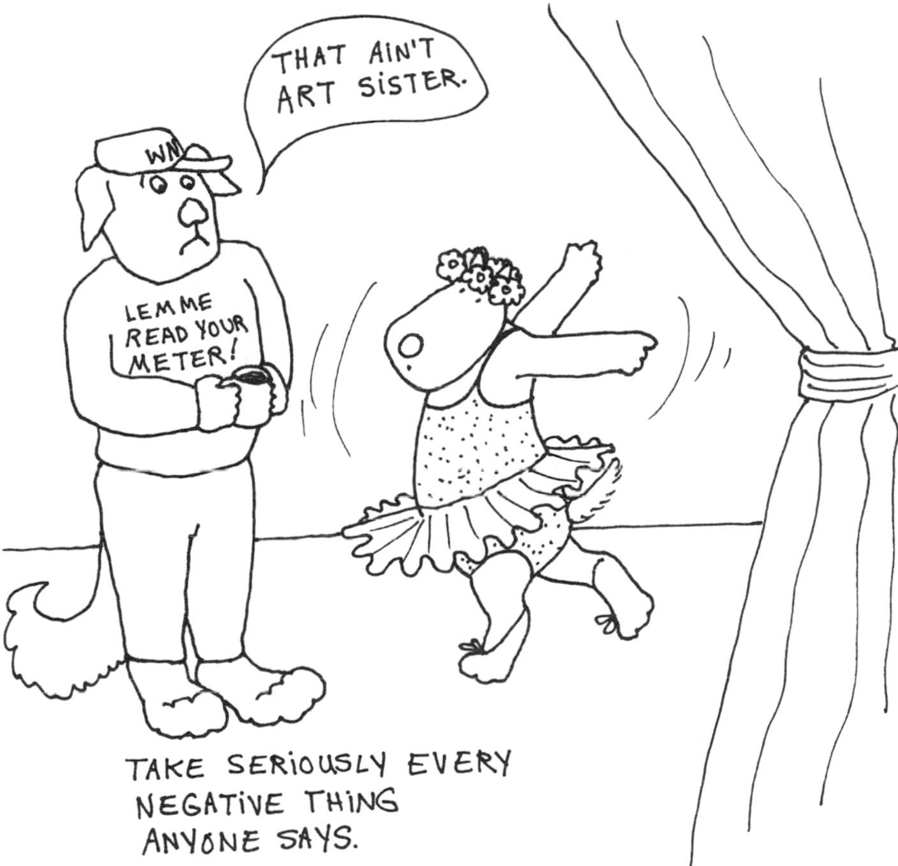
THAT AIN'T ART SISTER.
WM
LEMME READ YOUR METER!

TAKE SERIOUSLY EVERY NEGATIVE THING ANYONE SAYS.

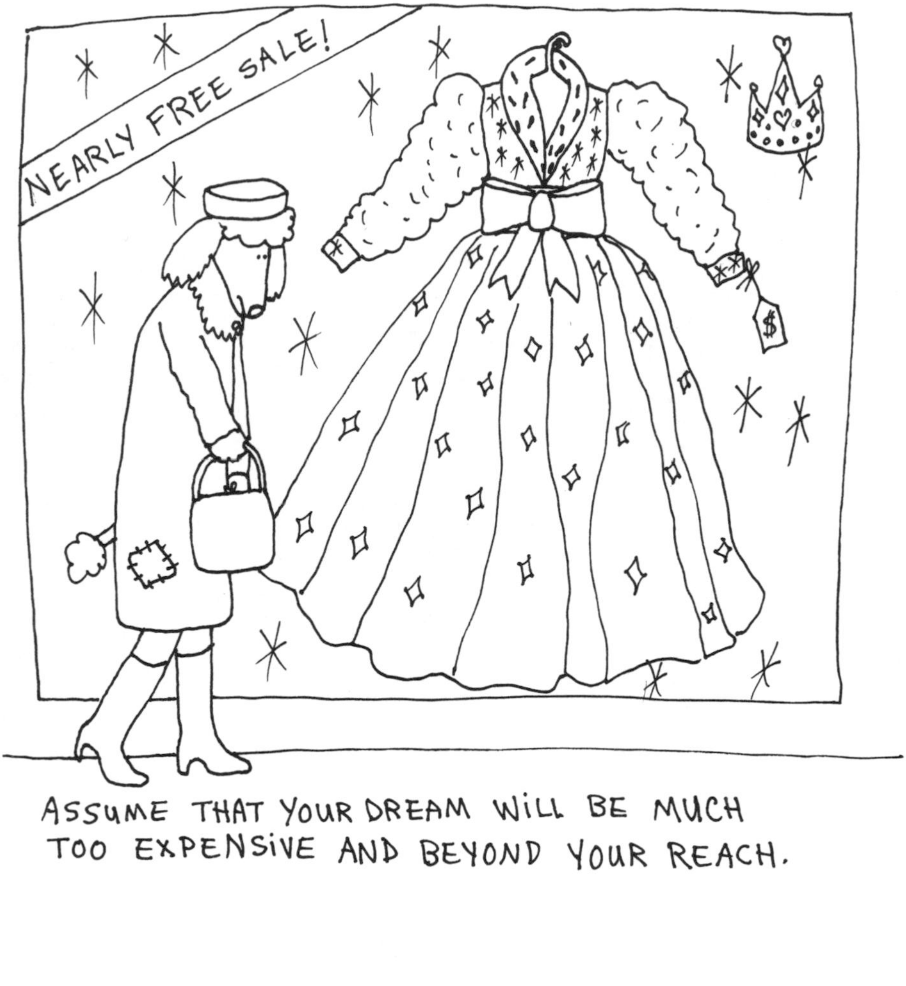
NEARLY FREE SALE!
$

ASSUME THAT YOUR DREAM WILL BE MUCH
TOO EXPENSIVE AND BEYOND YOUR REACH.

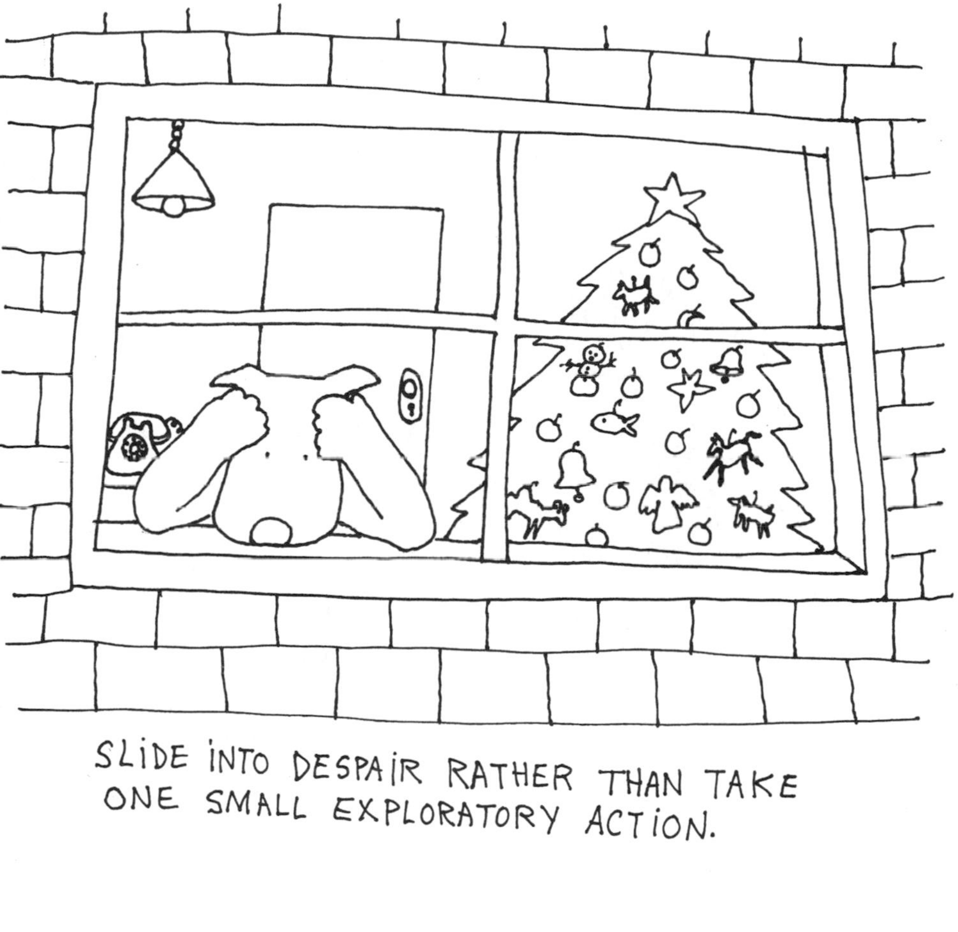

SLIDE INTO DESPAIR RATHER THAN TAKE ONE SMALL EXPLORATORY ACTION.

SURROUND YOURSELF
WITH JEALOUS,
BLOCKED, AND
NEGATIVE
COMPANIONS.

TALK ABOUT IT SO YOU DON'T HAVE TO DO IT.

OBSESS ABOUT HOW
PAINTING A TULIP MEANS
YOU ARE AN UNFIT
PARENT ABANDONING
YOUR CHILD TO PURSUE
YOUR SELFISH DREAM.

HELP SOMEONE ELSE MAKE THEIR ART.

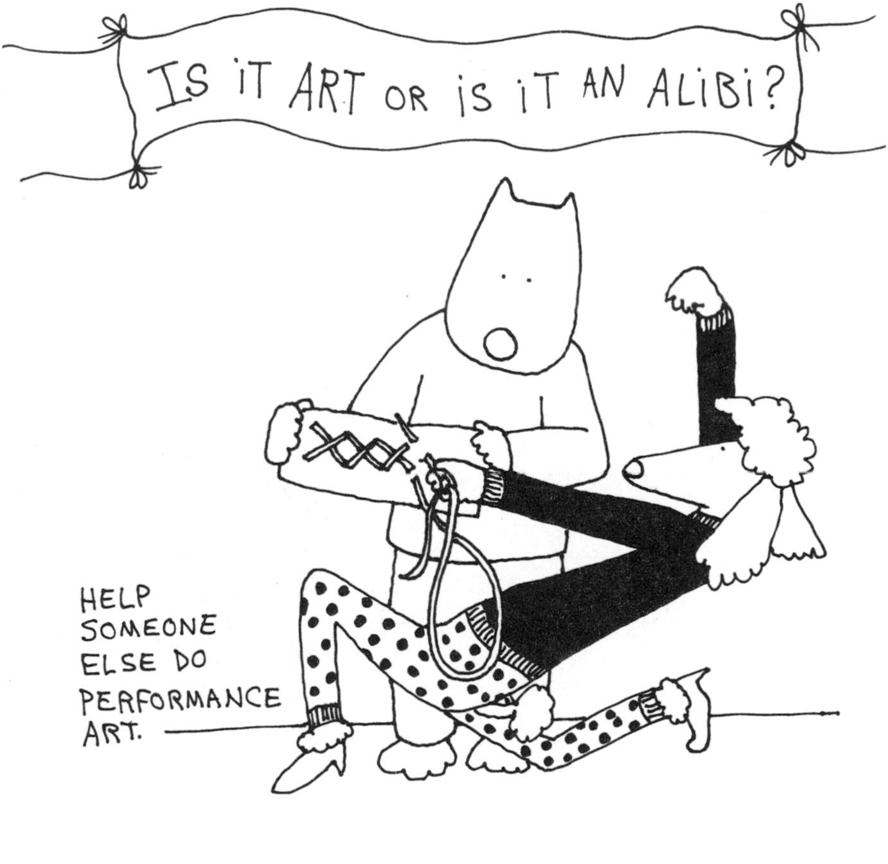
IS IT ART OR IS IT AN ALIBI?
HELP SOMEONE ELSE DO PERFORMANCE ART.

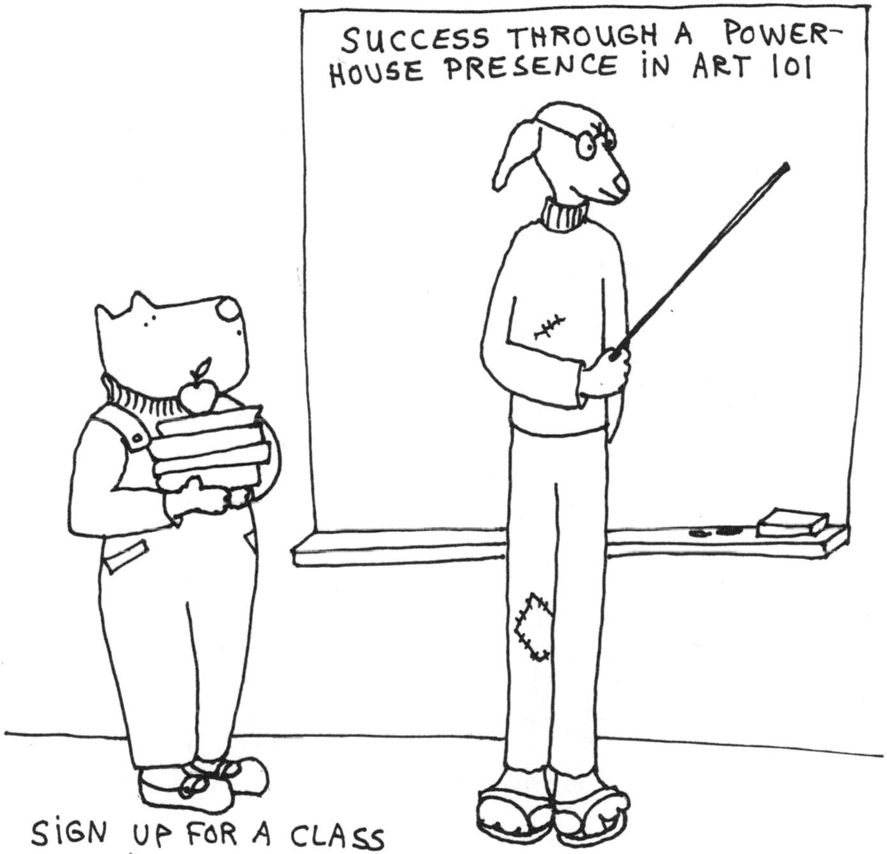
SUCCESS THROUGH A POWER-
HOUSE PRESENCE IN ART 101

SIGN UP FOR A CLASS
WITH A TEACHER WHO IS AN "EXPERT" ALTHOUGH
HE'S NEVER MADE ANYTHING MUCH HIMSELF.

CONSIDER THE ODDS AGAINST WHATEVER YOU MAKE EVER SELLING.

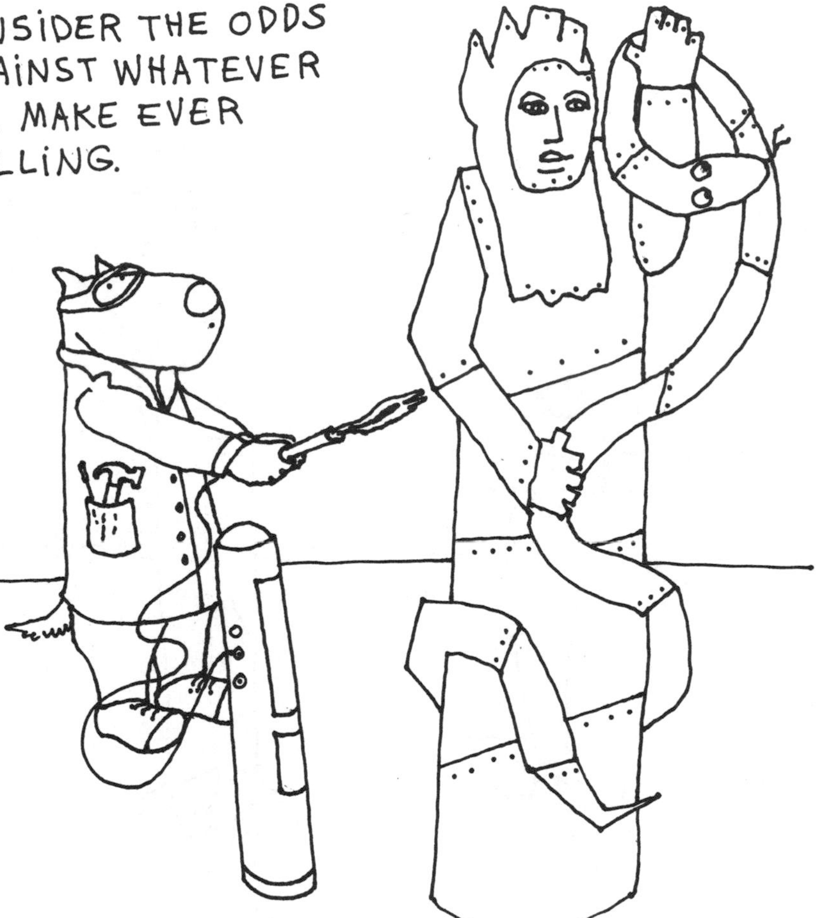

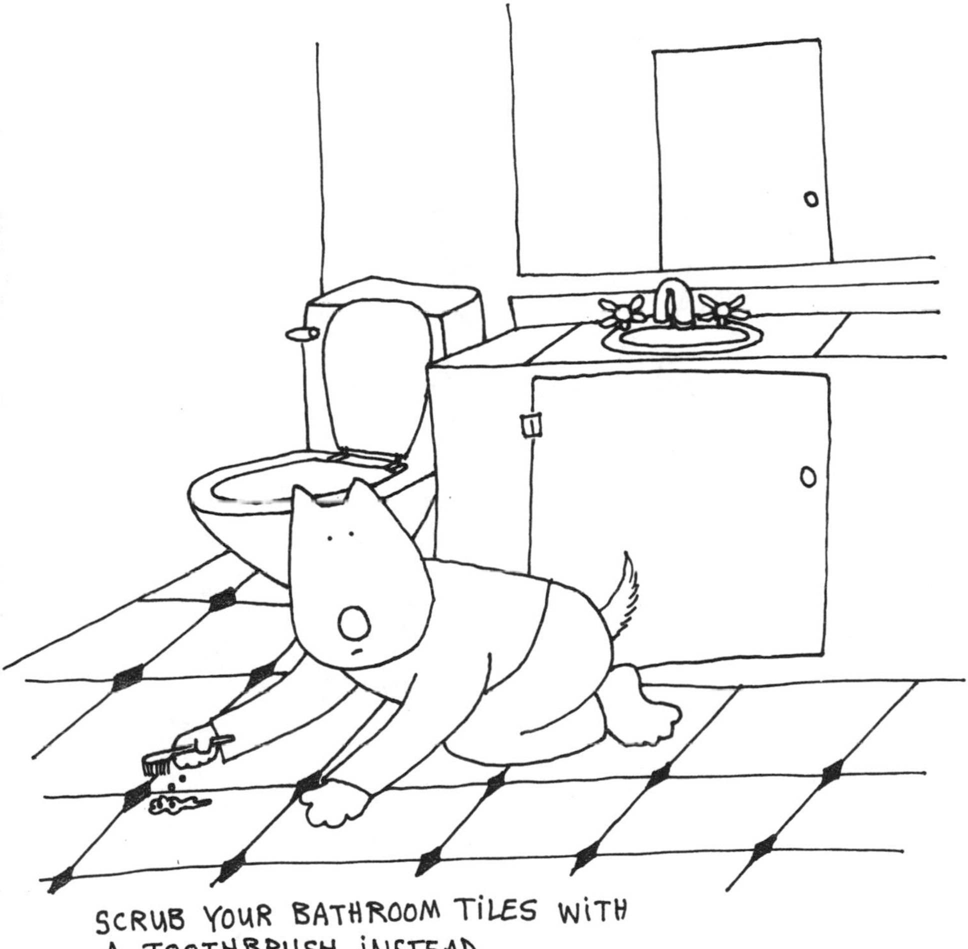

SCRUB YOUR BATHROOM TILES WITH A TOOTHBRUSH INSTEAD.

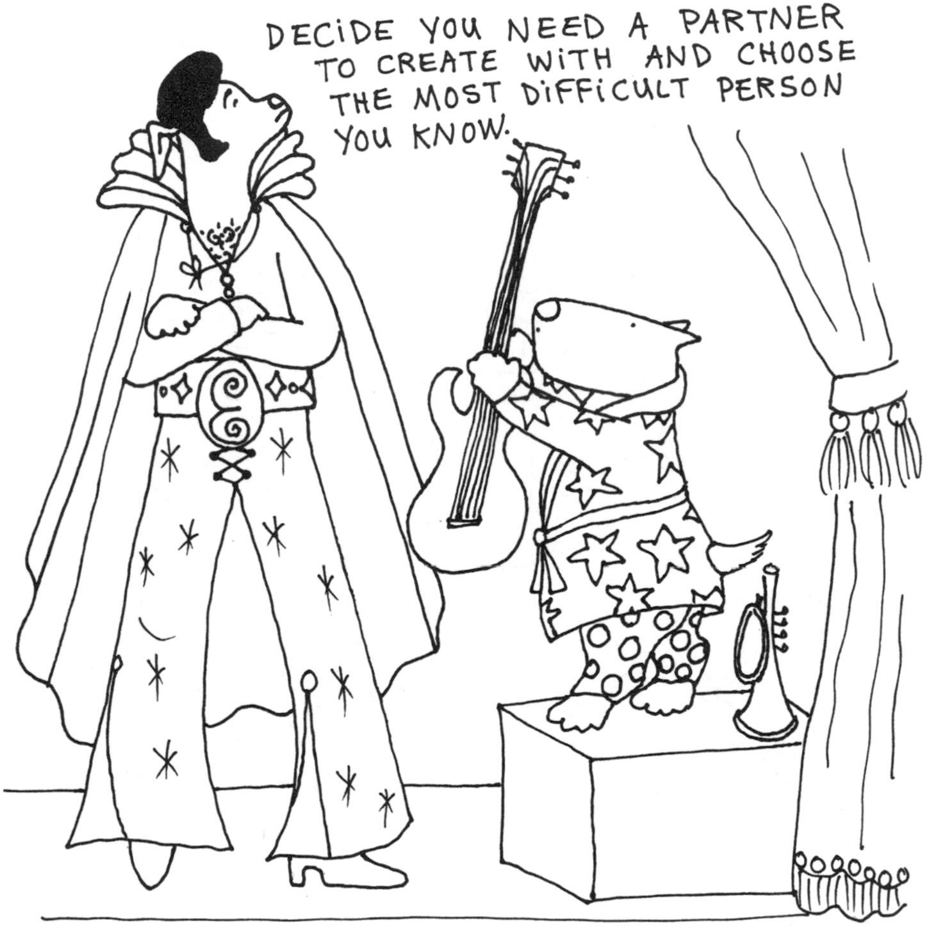
DECIDE YOU NEED A PARTNER TO CREATE WITH AND CHOOSE THE MOST DIFFICULT PERSON YOU KNOW.

TELL YOUR MOST NEGATIVE SIBLING YOUR DREAM AND THEN LISTEN TO THEIR REASONS WHY YOU SHOULDN'T DO IT.

CALL YOUR MOST JEALOUS FRIEND.

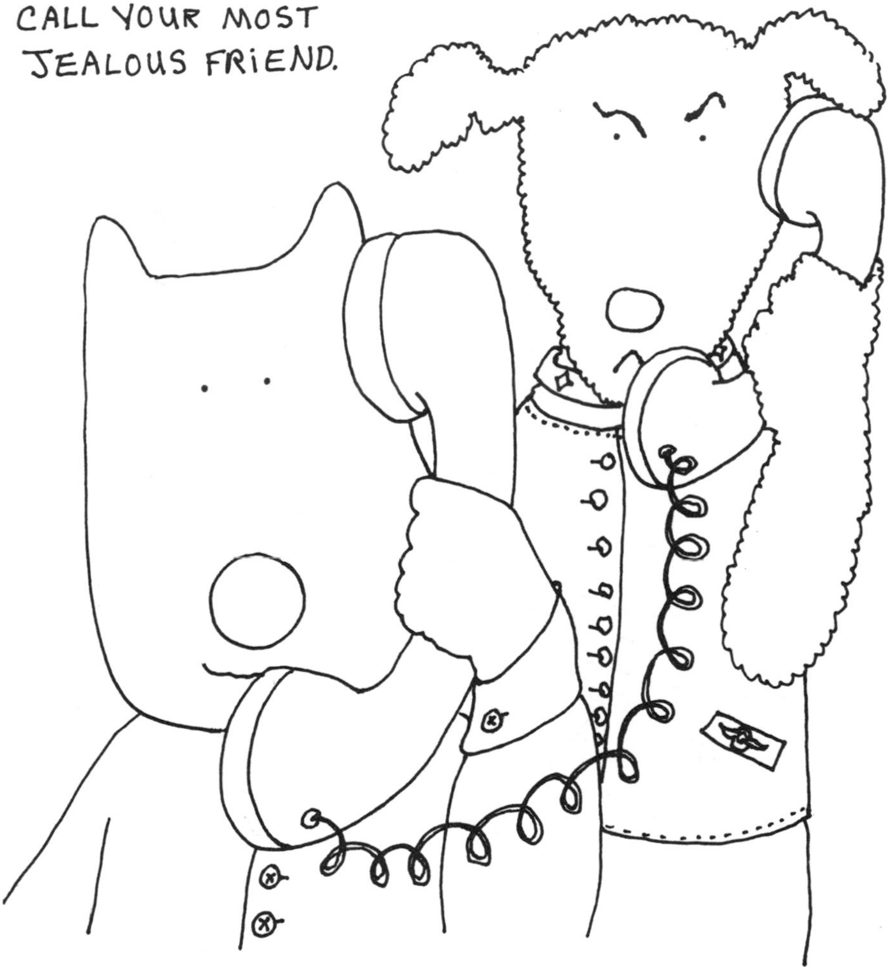

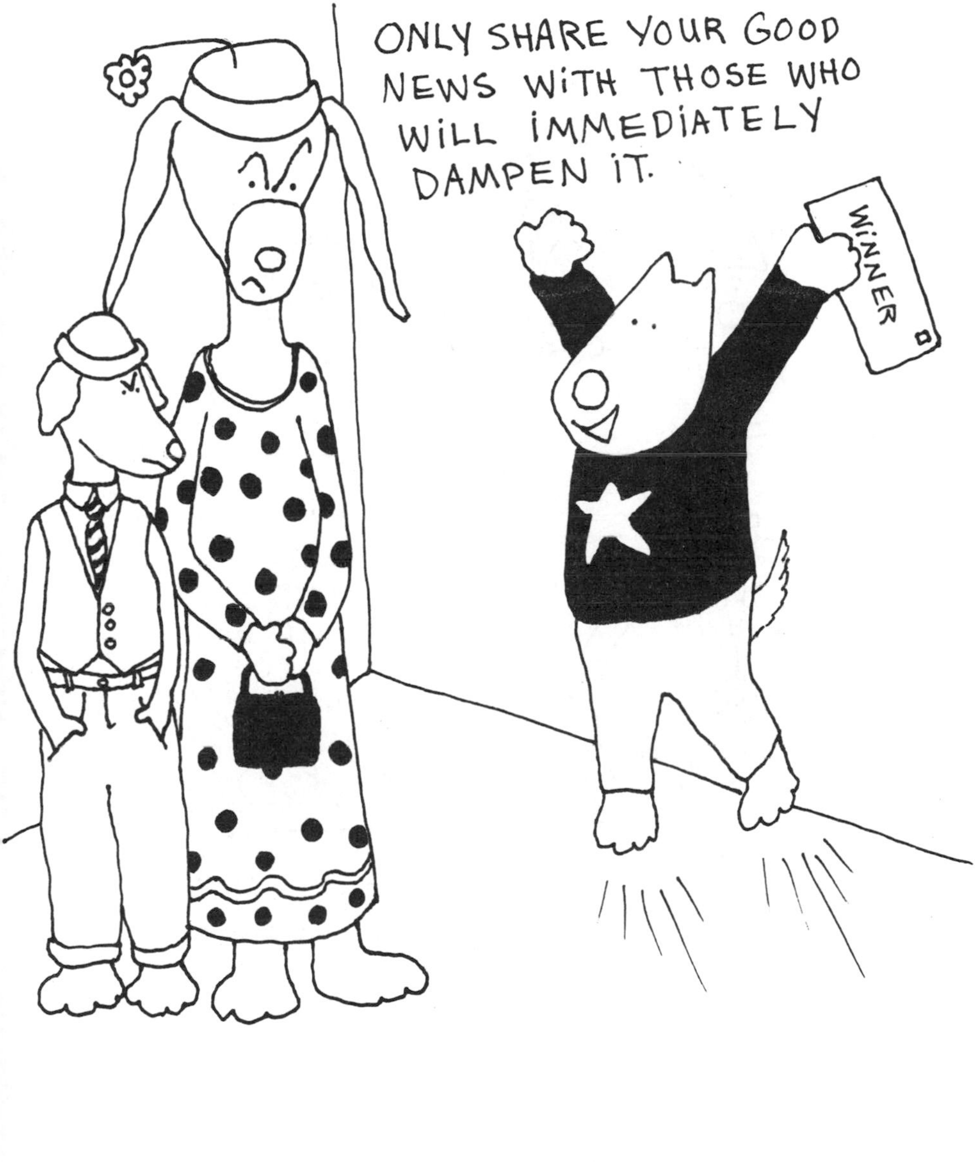
ONLY SHARE YOUR GOOD NEWS WITH THOSE WHO WILL IMMEDIATELY DAMPEN IT.
WINNER

DEMAND THAT WHAT YOU DO BE ABSOLUTELY ORIGINAL, TOTALLY BRILLIANT, AND NEVER DONE BEFORE.

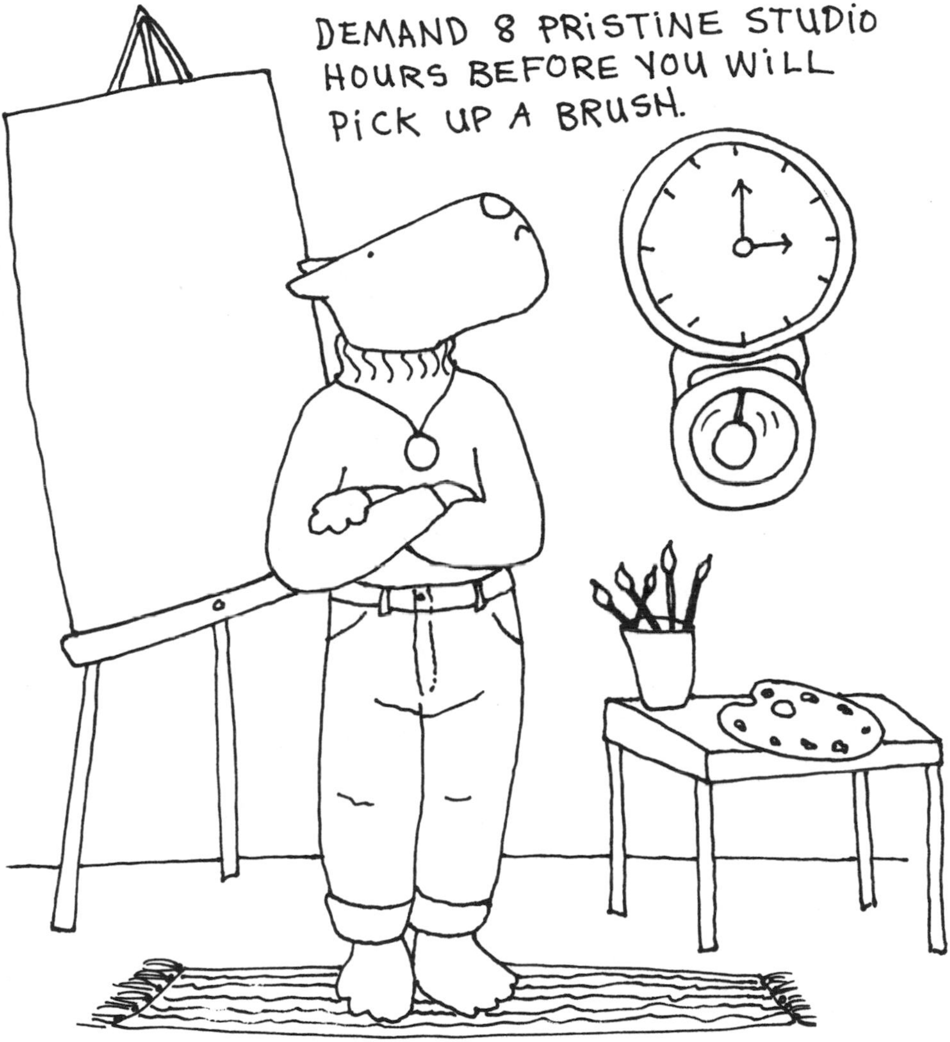
DEMAND 8 PRISTINE STUDIO HOURS BEFORE YOU WILL PICK UP A BRUSH.

DEVOTE EVERY MINUTE TO A MENIAL
JOB SO YOU HAVE NO TIME OR ENERGY
FOR YOUR ART.

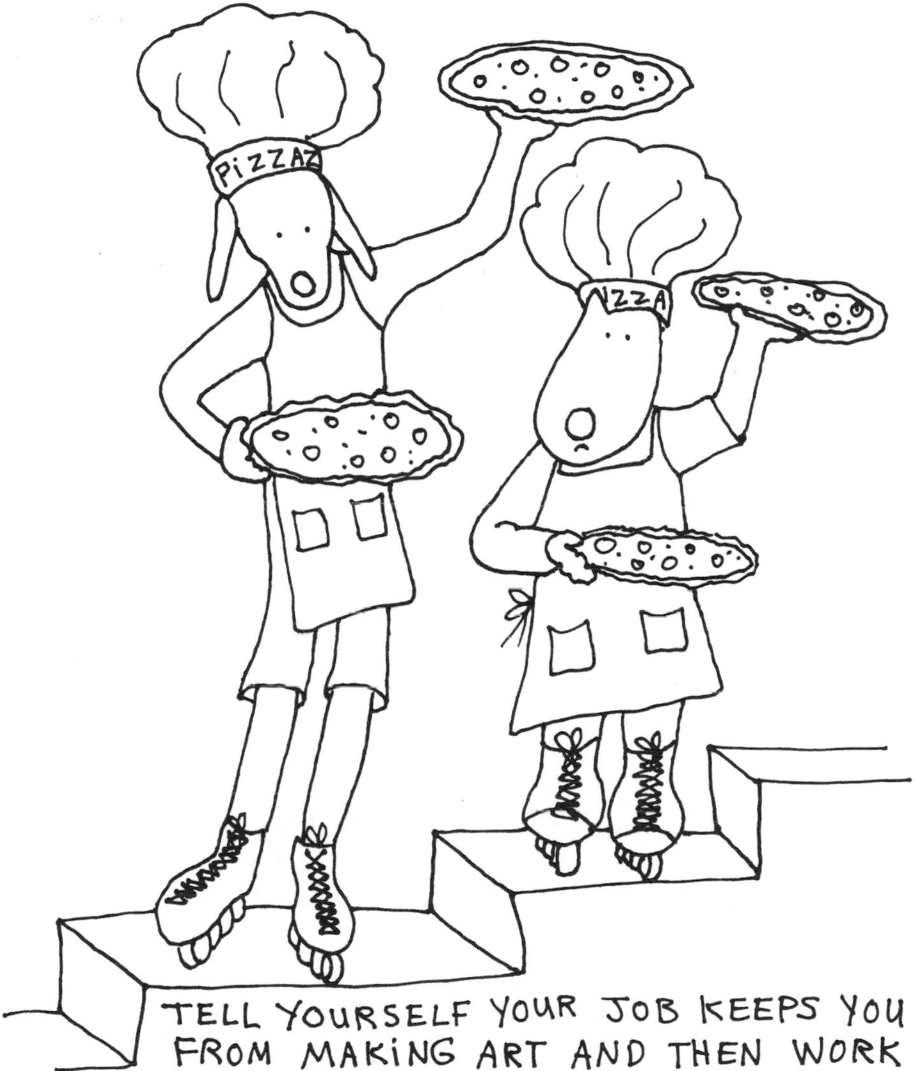
PiZZAZ
IZZA

TELL YOURSELF YOUR JOB KEEPS YOU FROM MAKiNG ART AND THEN WORK OVERTiME JUST TO PROVE iT.

DEMAND 15 HOURS OF FREE TIME TO CREATE, SO YOU CAN IGNORE THE 15 MINUTES YOU'VE GOT.

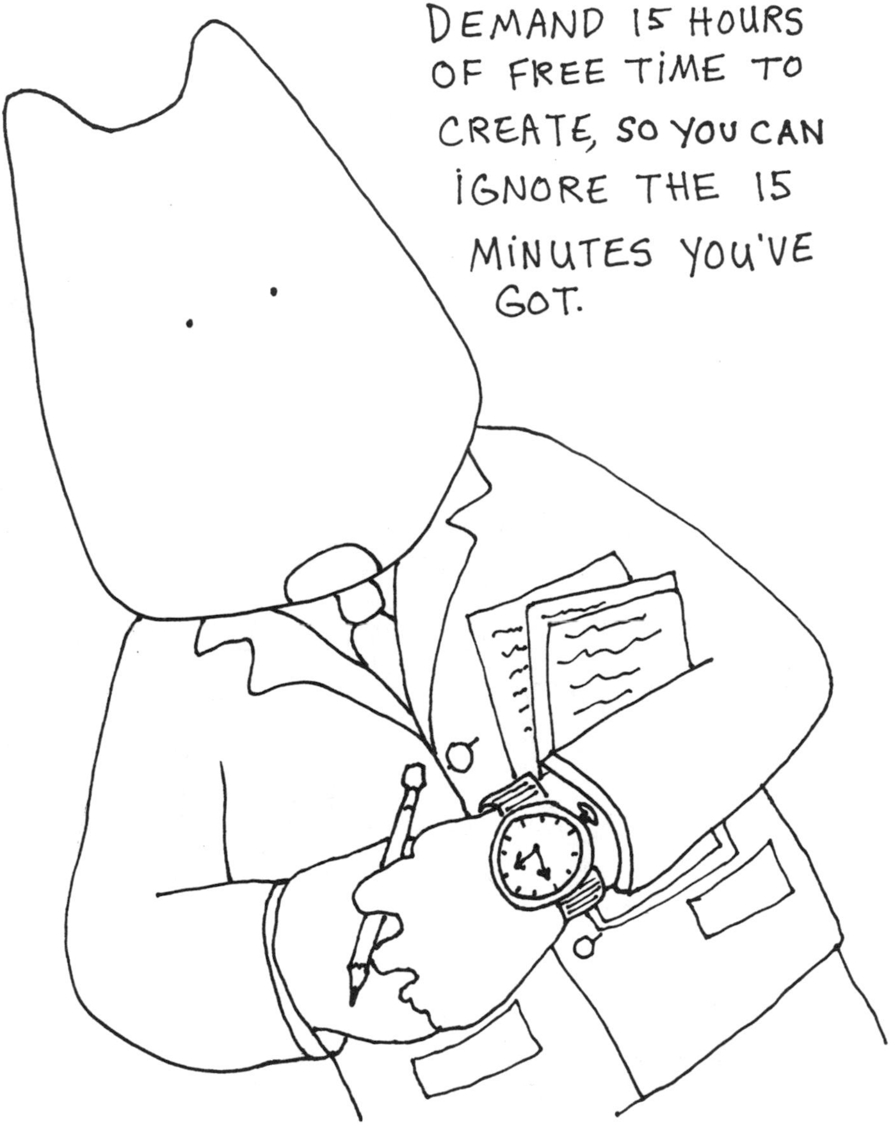

ACQUIRE A HIGH MAINTENANCE RELATIONSHIP.

CHOOSE SOMEONE WHO FEELS THEIR DREAMS AND GOALS ARE FAR MORE IMPORTANT THAN YOURS

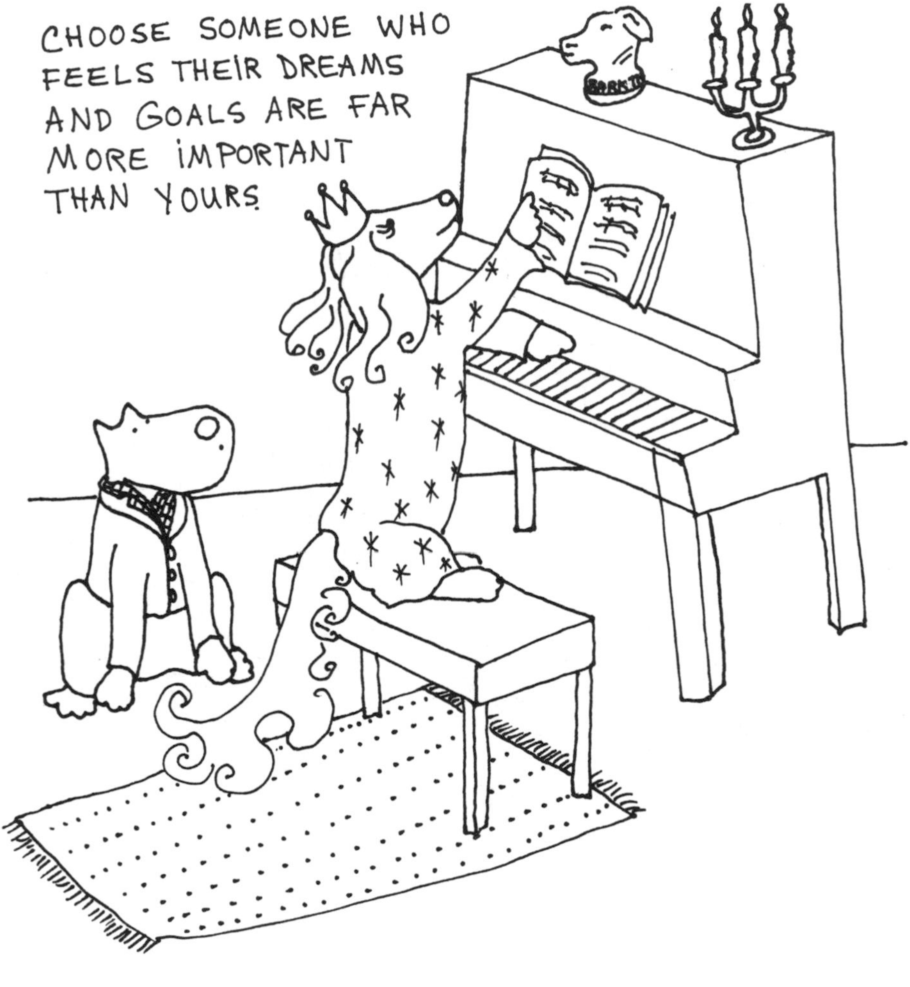

VOLUNTEER TO BE THEIR SOUNDING BOARD AND
ADVISOR, INSTEAD OF GETTING YOUR WORK DONE.

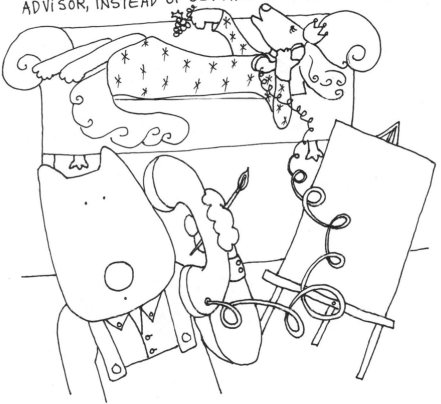

HELP OTHERS TO FORMULATE A STEP-BY-STEP APPROACH FOR MANIFESTING *THEIR* DREAMS.

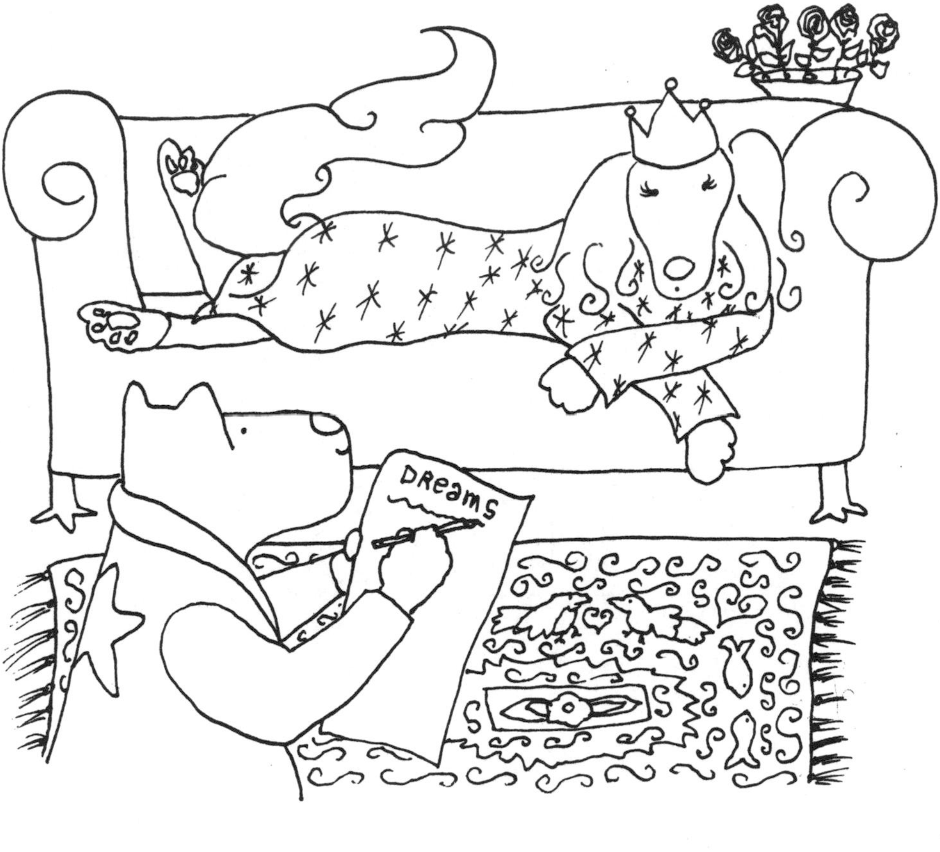
DReams

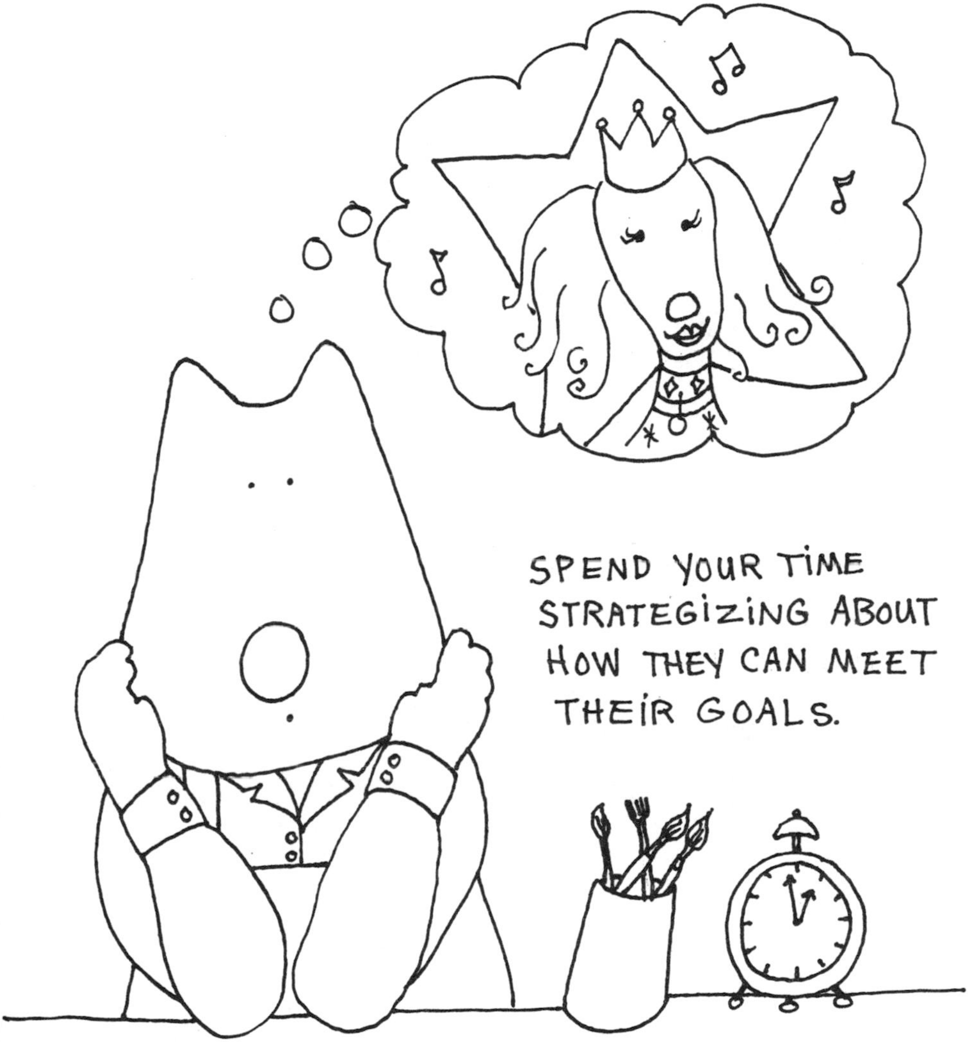

SPEND YOUR TIME STRATEGIZING ABOUT HOW THEY CAN MEET THEIR GOALS.

KEEP YOUR
RADAR TUNED
FOR THEIR
CAREER
OPPORTUNITIES.
IGNORE YOURS.

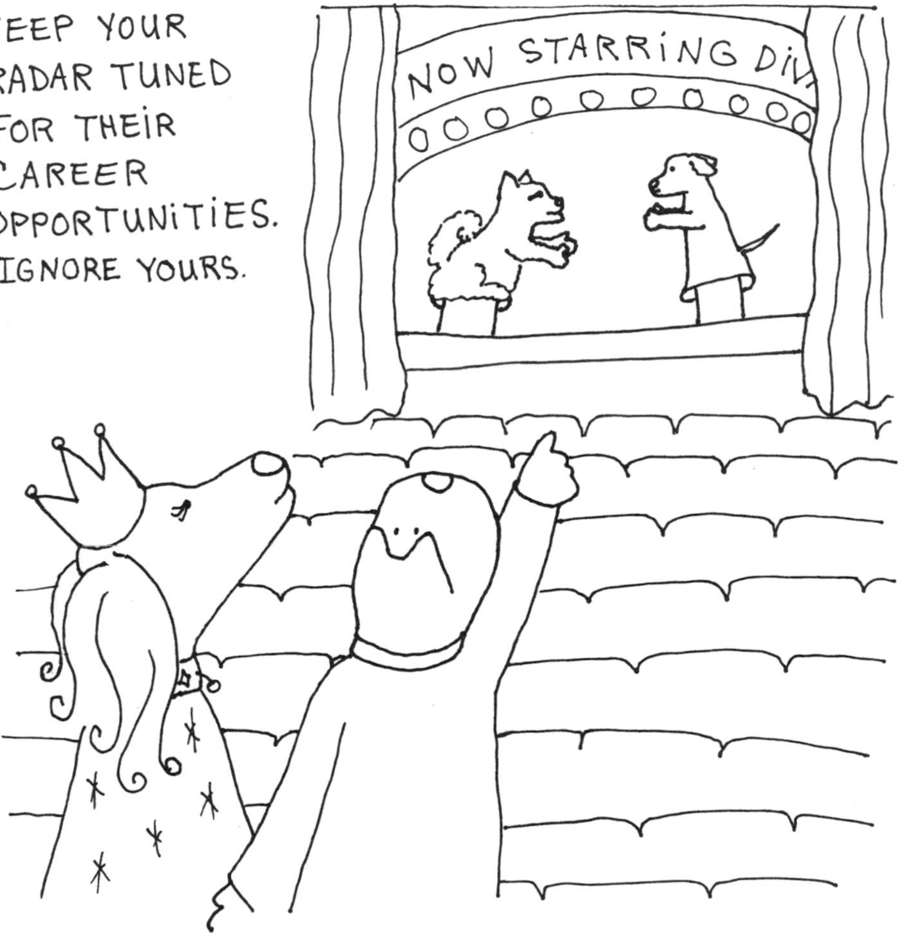
NOW STARRING DIV

BANKROLL THEIR ENDEAVORS
AND CALL IT INVESTING IN THE RELATIONSHIP.

MAKE IT A RULE TO TABLE YOUR WORK AND YOUR DEADLINES WHENEVER THEY NEED YOUR FOCUS ON THEIRS.

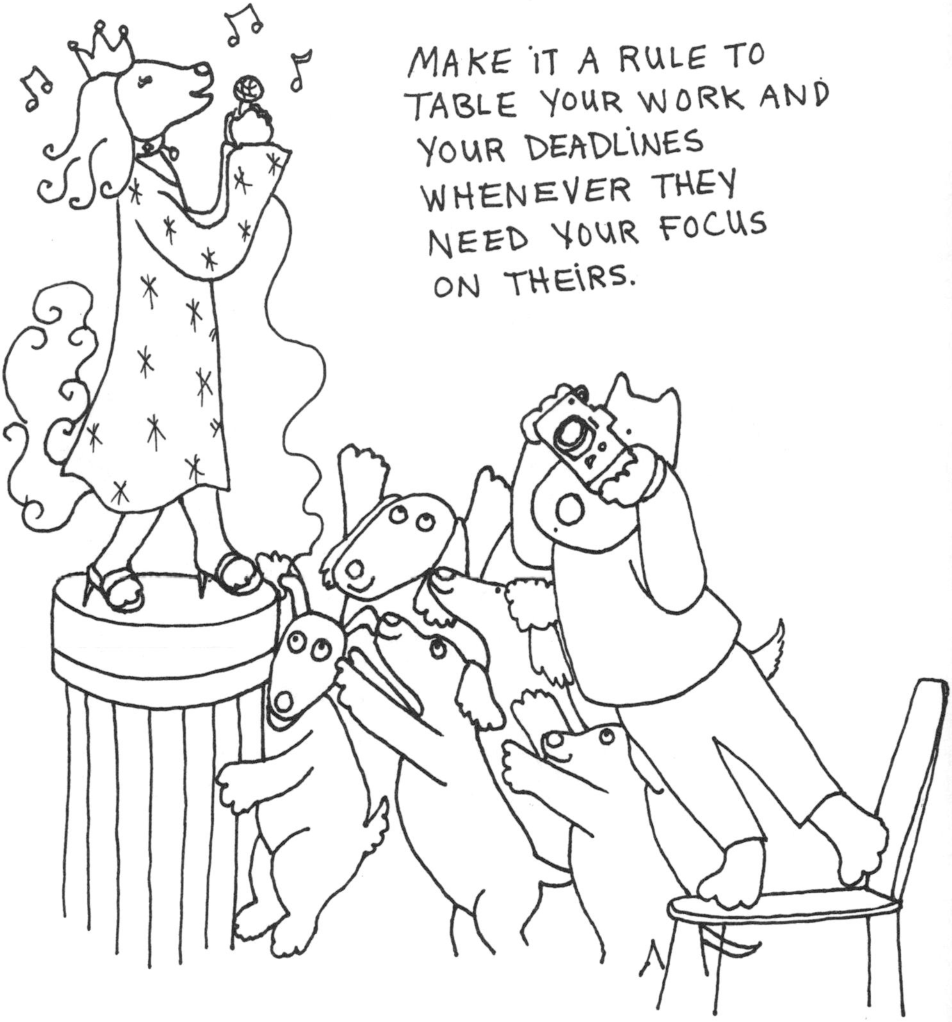

IF THEY HAVE A FIT BECAUSE YOUR FOCUS ON THEM WAVERS EVEN FOR A MINUTE, TELL YOURSELF THEIR GOALS REALLY ARE THAT IMPORTANT.

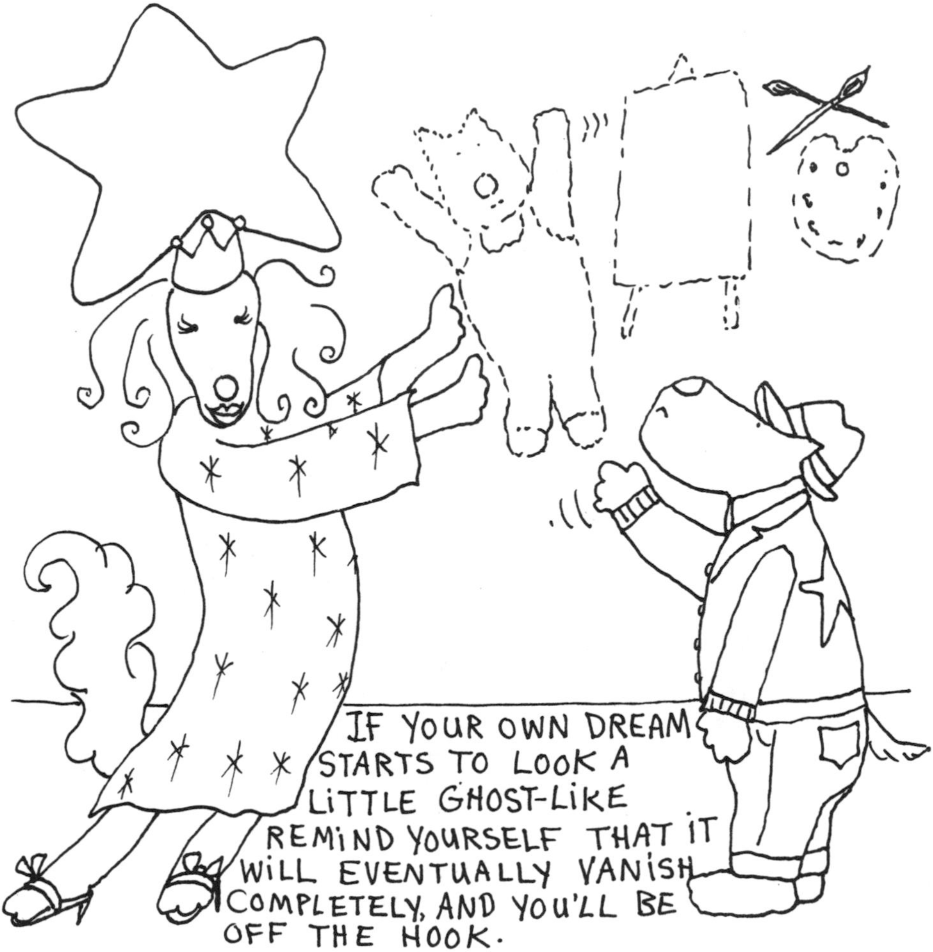
IF YOUR OWN DREAM STARTS TO LOOK A LITTLE GHOST-LIKE REMIND YOURSELF THAT IT WILL EVENTUALLY VANISH COMPLETELY, AND YOU'LL BE OFF THE HOOK.

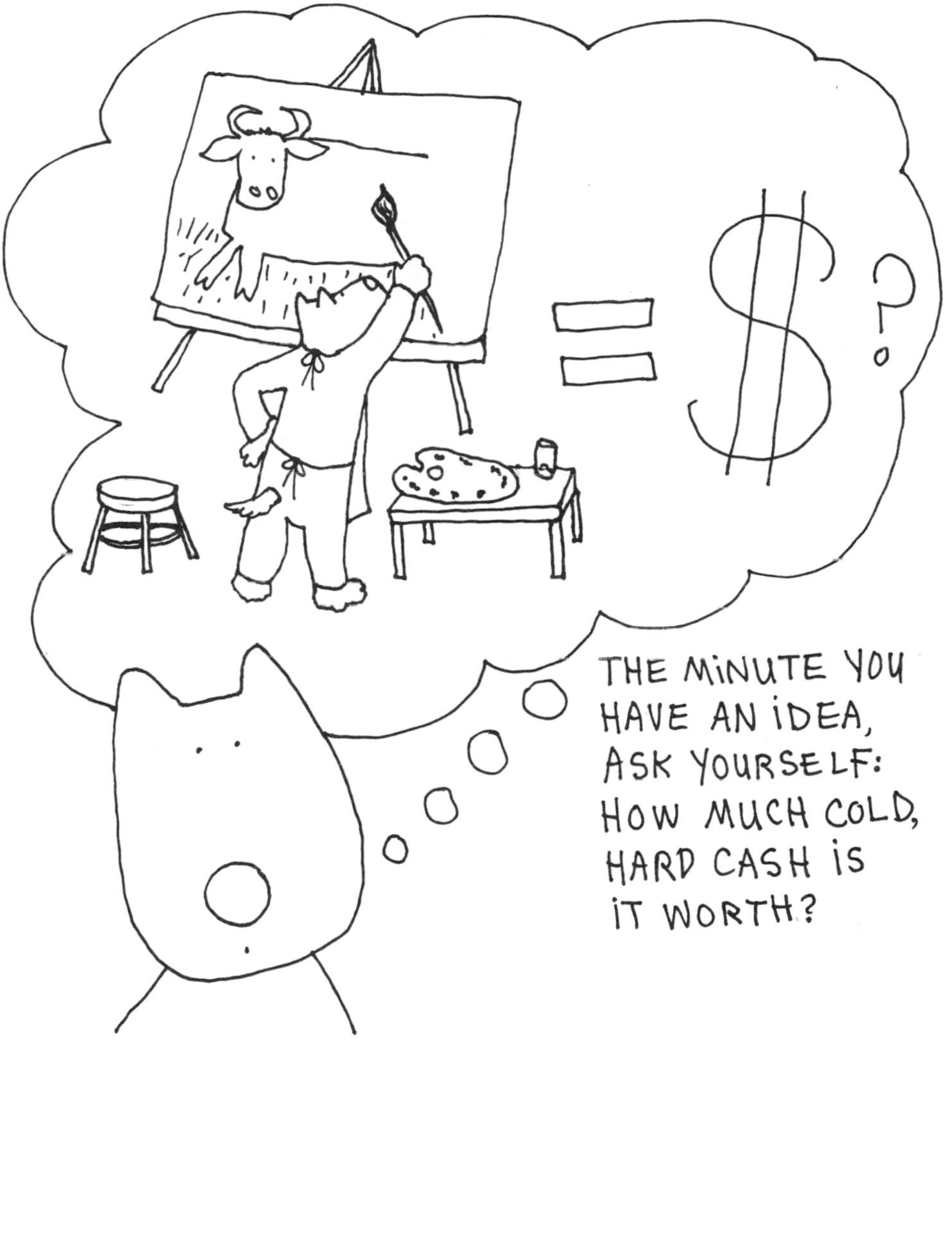
THE MINUTE YOU HAVE AN IDEA, ASK YOURSELF: HOW MUCH COLD, HARD CASH IS IT WORTH?

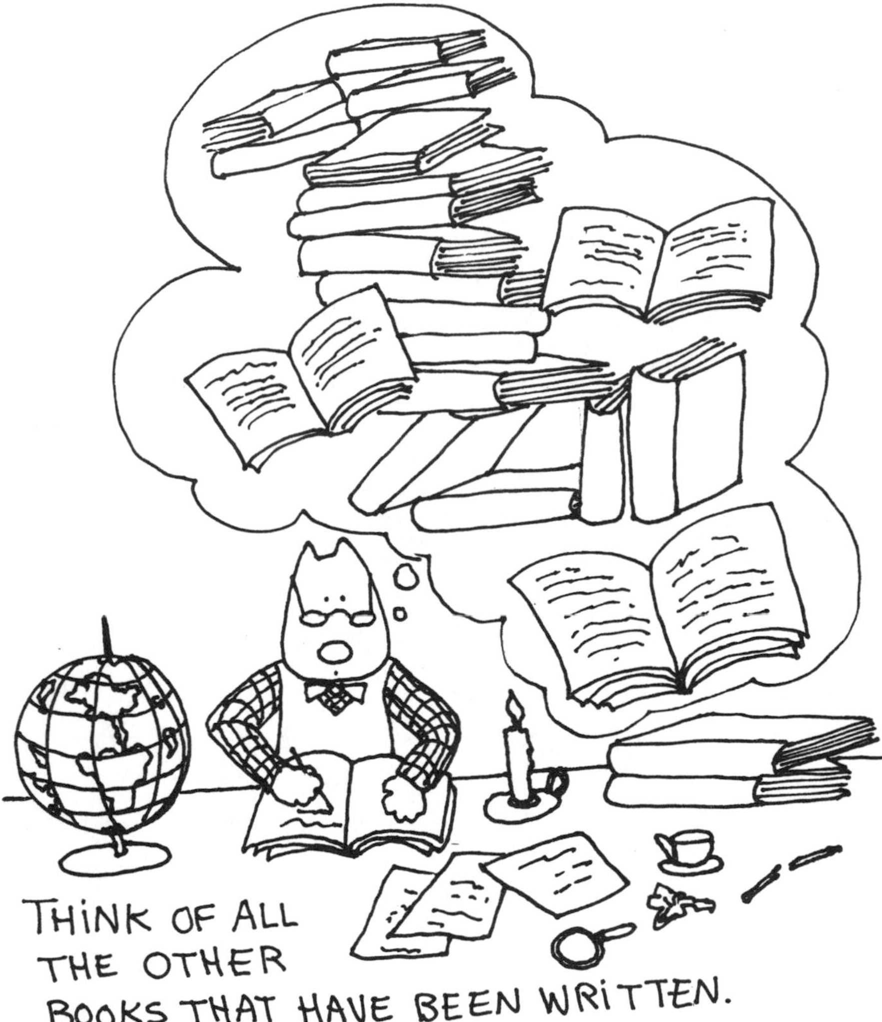
THINK OF ALL
THE OTHER
BOOKS THAT HAVE BEEN WRITTEN.
WHY WRITE THIS ONE?

TELL YOURSELF
YOU'RE TOO
OLD TO DO
THE THINGS
YOU
LOVE.

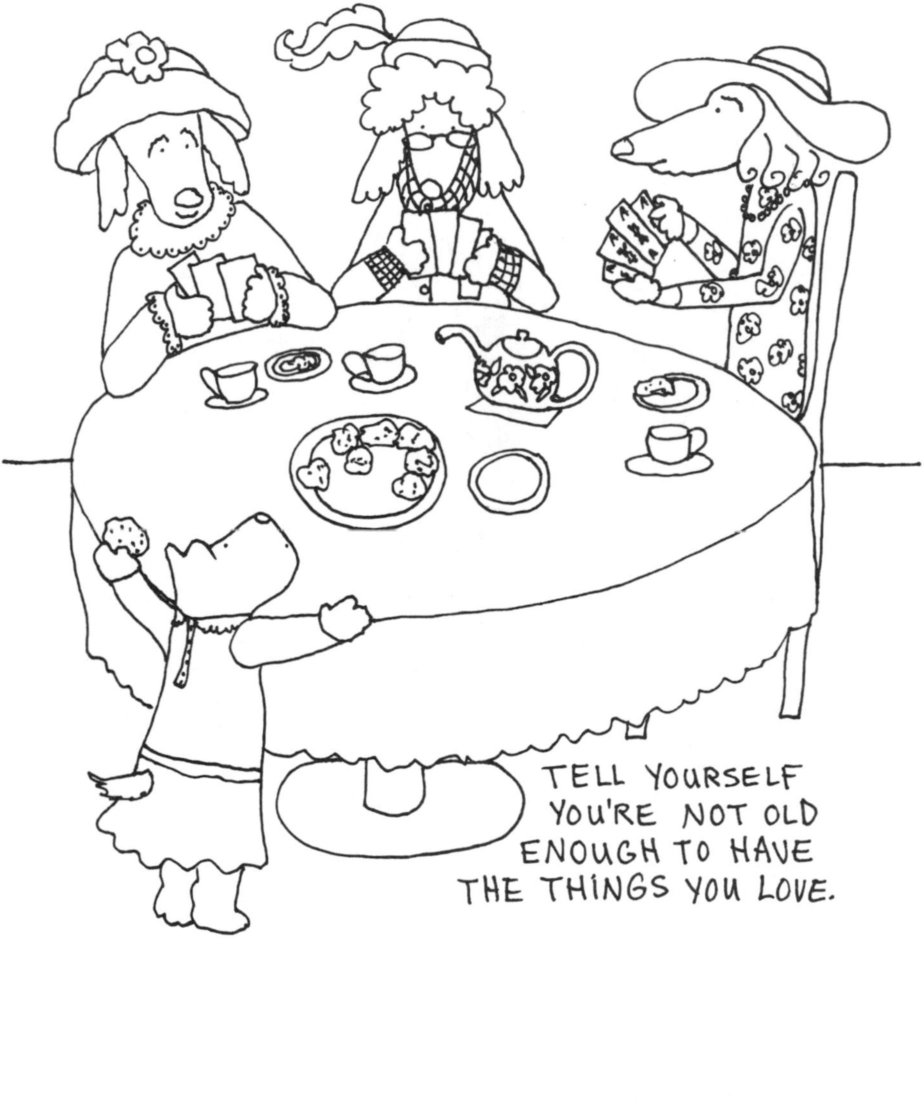

TELL YOURSELF
YOU'RE NOT OLD
ENOUGH TO HAVE
THE THINGS YOU LOVE.

WATCH T.V.
INSTEAD OF
THE MOVIE
IN YOUR MIND.

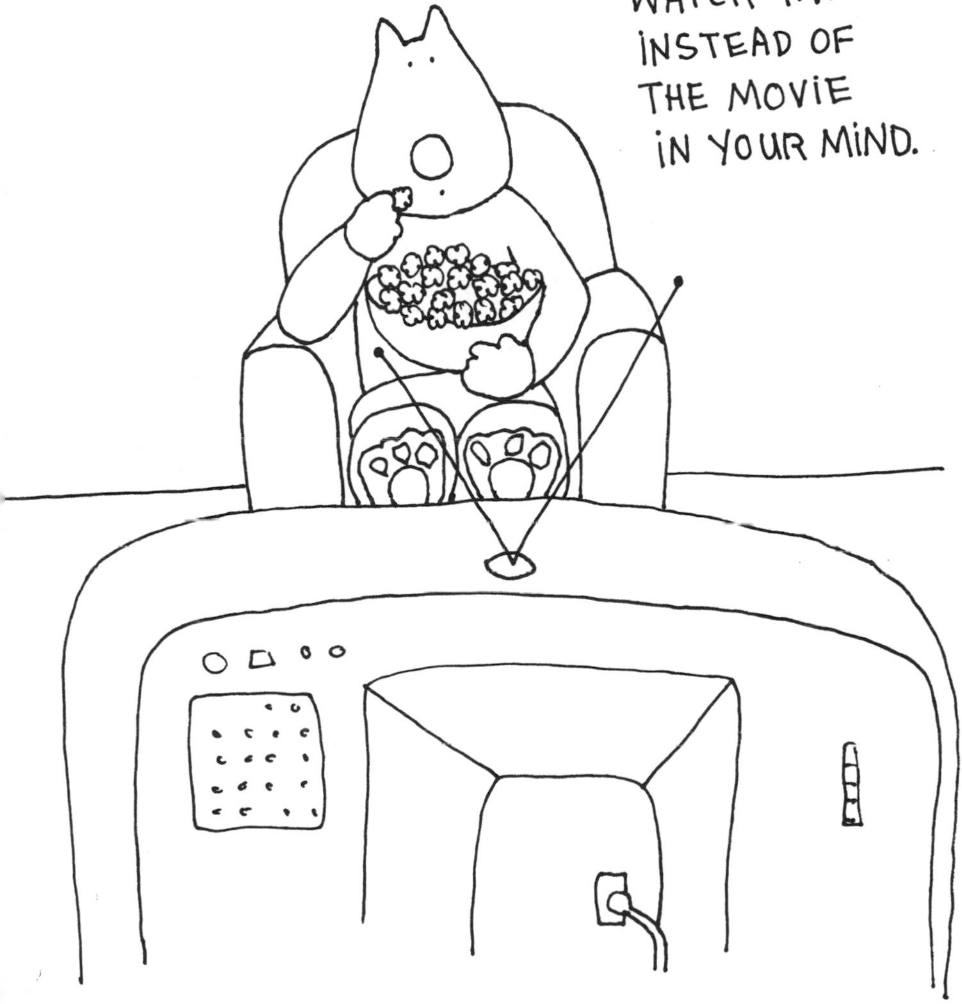

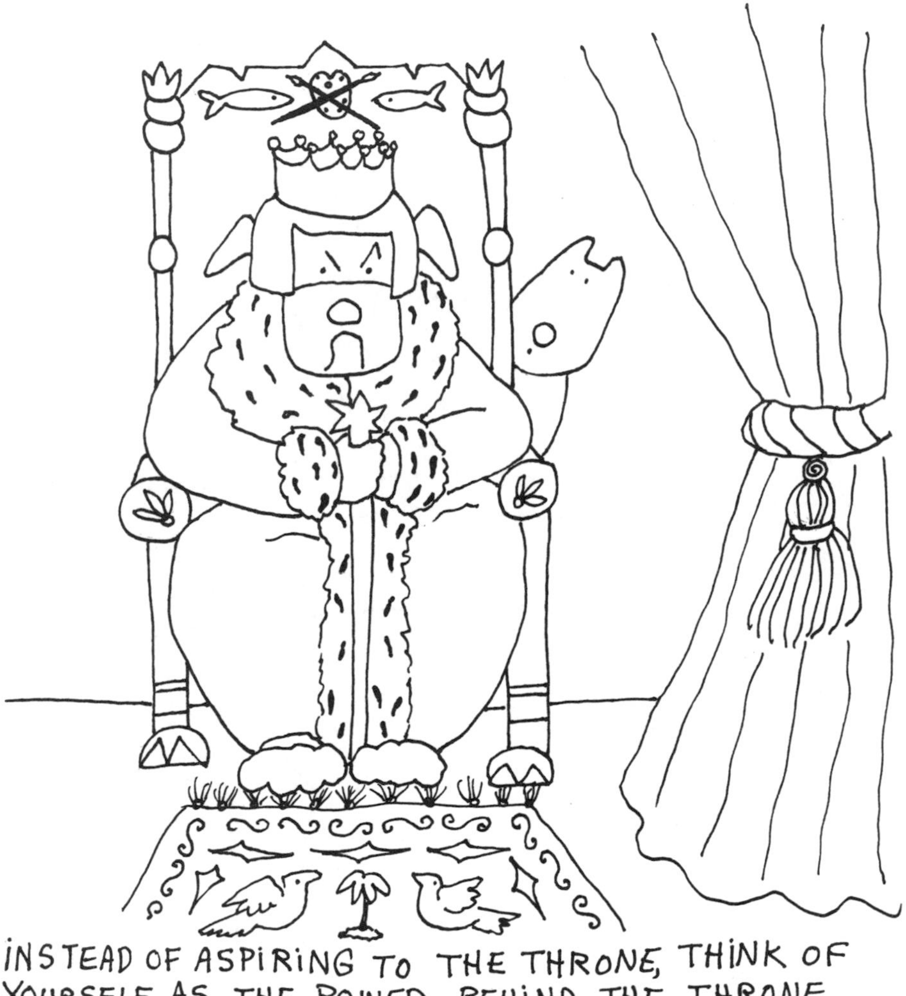

INSTEAD OF ASPIRING TO THE THRONE, THINK OF YOURSELF AS THE POWER BEHIND THE THRONE.

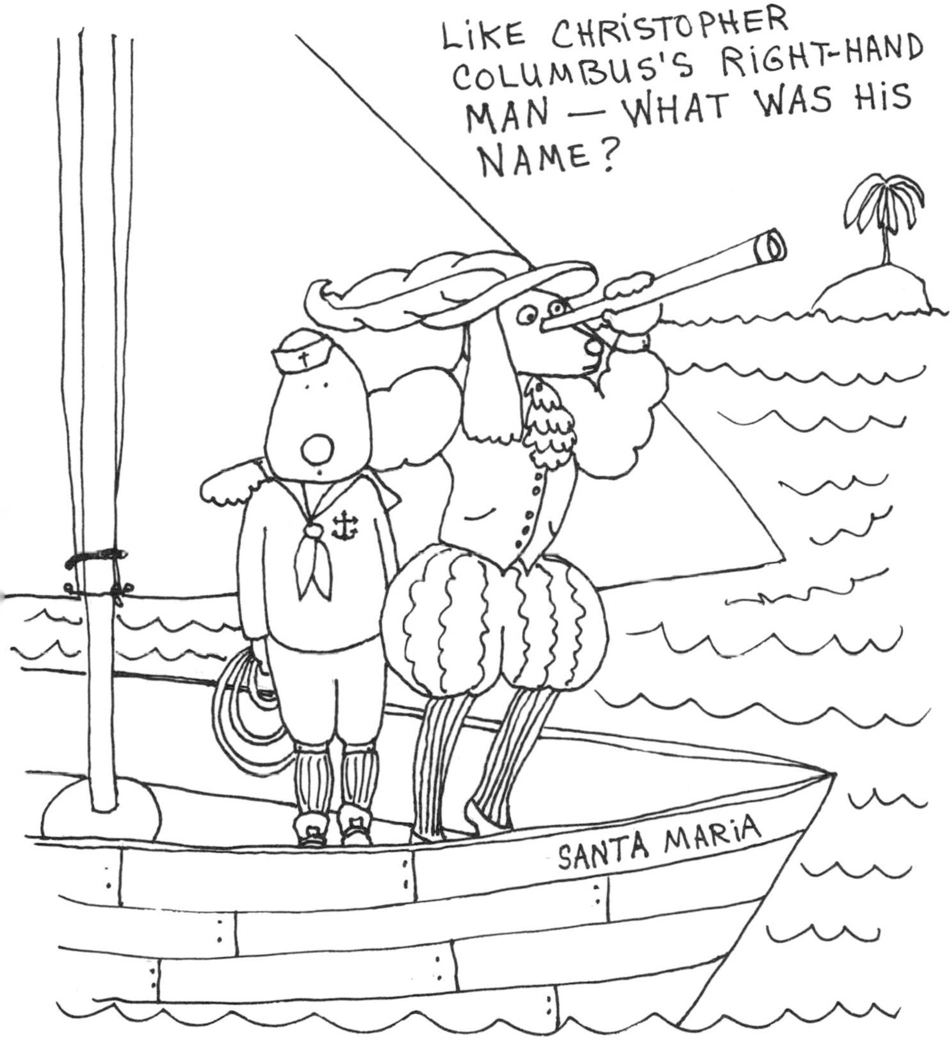
LIKE CHRISTOPHER COLUMBUS'S RIGHT-HAND MAN — WHAT WAS HIS NAME?
SANTA MARIA

WHEN YOUR BOSS PUTS MORE BRICKS IN YOUR PACK, FEEL CRAZY THAT YOU CAN'T KEEP UP.

HIRE "HELPLESS" HELPERS
WHO DRAIN YOU OF YOUR
CREATIVE ENERGY.

RESENTMENTS ARE HEAVY NO MATTER HOW MUCH YOU LOVE THE OFFENDERS. COLLECT AS MANY AS POSSIBLE.

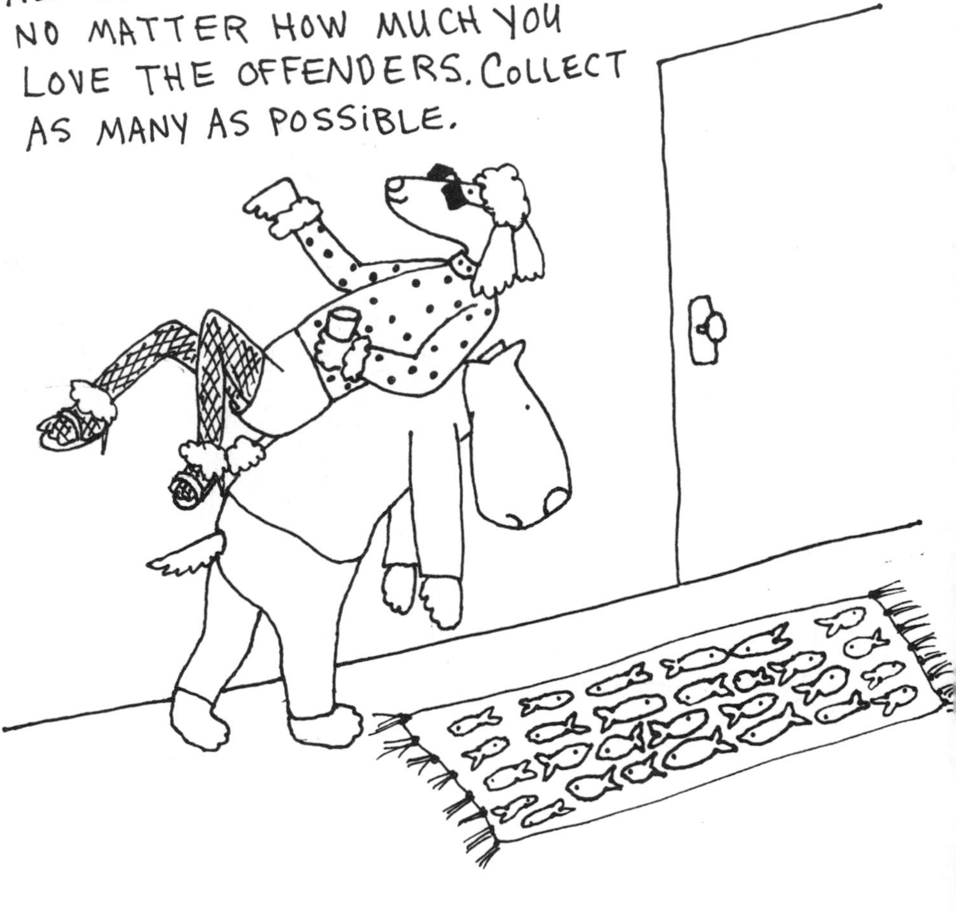

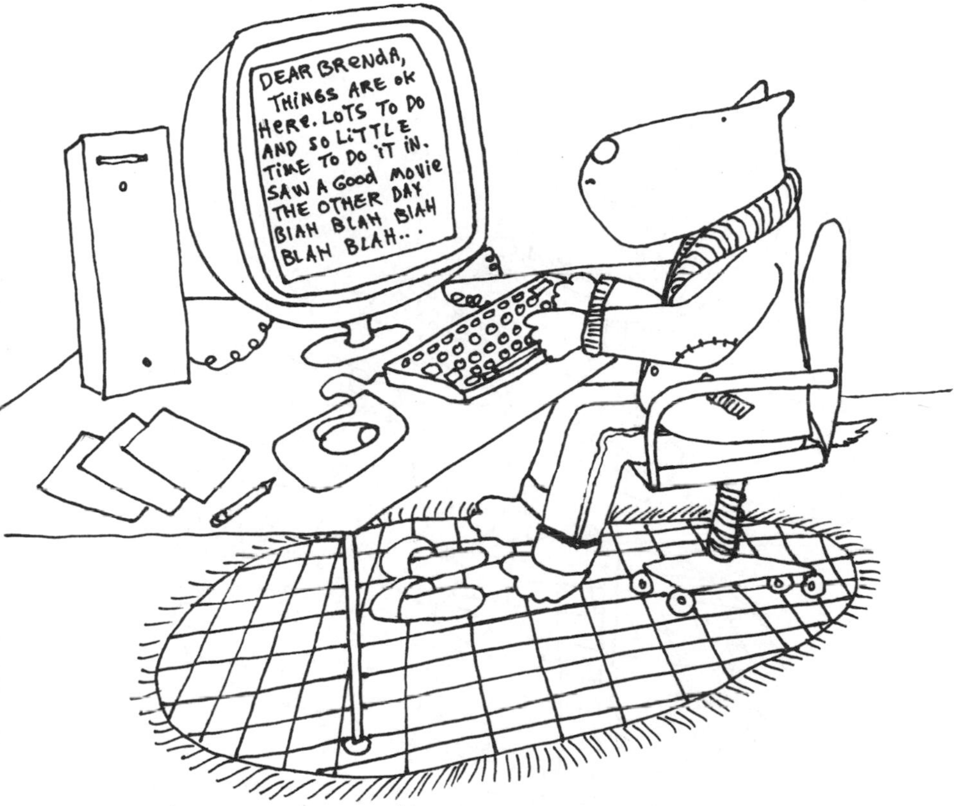
DEAR BRENDA,
THINGS ARE OK
HERE. LOTS TO DO
AND SO LITTLE
TIME TO DO IT IN.
SAW A GOOD MOVIE
THE OTHER DAY
BLAH BLAH BLAH
BLAH BLAH...

WRITE LONG EMAILS TO YOUR FRIENDS,
INSTEAD OF WRITING YOUR NOVEL.

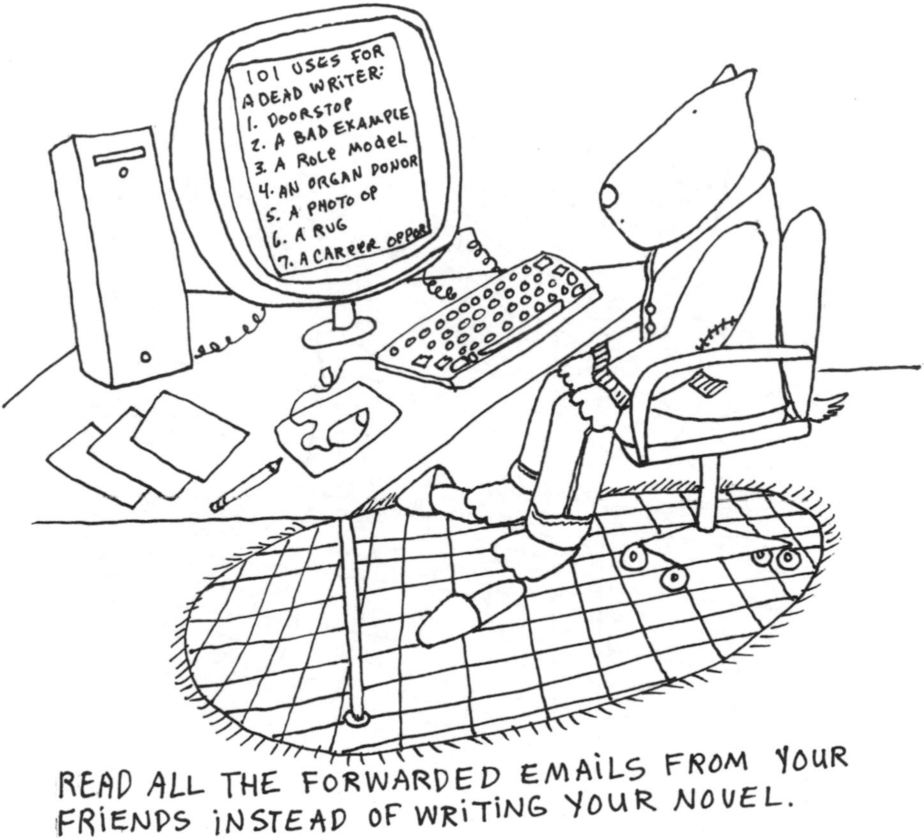
101 USES FOR
A DEAD WRITER:
1. DOORSTOP
2. A BAD EXAMPLE
3. A ROLE MODEL
4. AN ORGAN DONOR
5. A PHOTO OP
6. A RUG
7. A CAREER OPPOR

READ ALL THE FORWARDED EMAILS FROM YOUR FRIENDS INSTEAD OF WRITING YOUR NOVEL.

COOK AN ELABORATE,
FATTENING, TIME CONSUMING
DINNER THAT NO ONE REALLY WANTS
OR NEEDS, SO YOU CAN STAY AWAY
FROM THE DREADED EASEL.

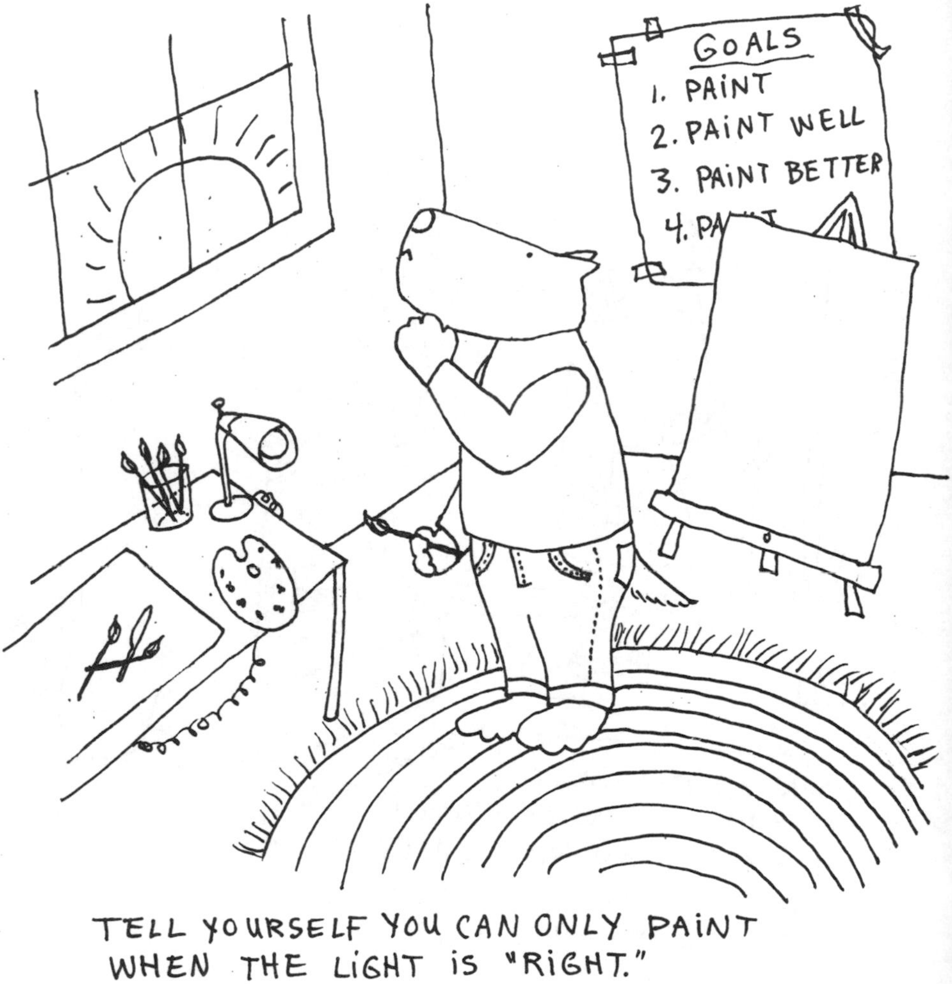
GOALS
1. PAINT
2. PAINT WELL
3. PAINT BETTER

TELL YOURSELF YOU CAN ONLY PAINT WHEN THE LIGHT IS "RIGHT."

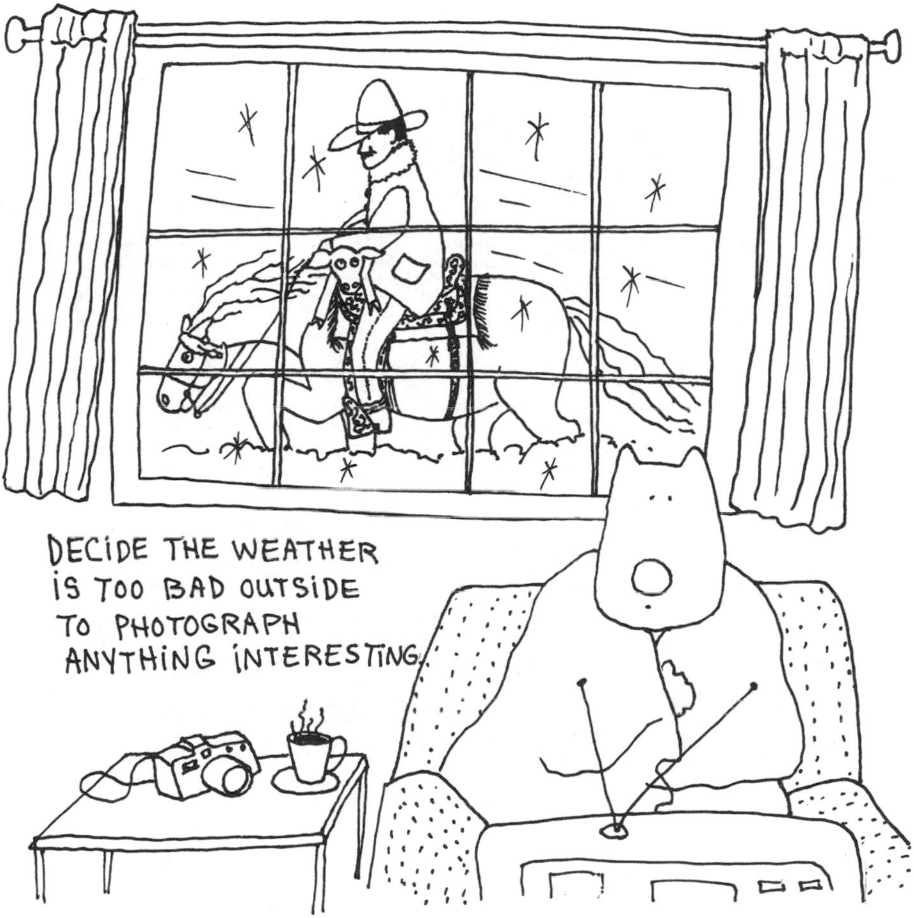
DECIDE THE WEATHER
IS TOO BAD OUTSIDE
TO PHOTOGRAPH
ANYTHING INTERESTING.

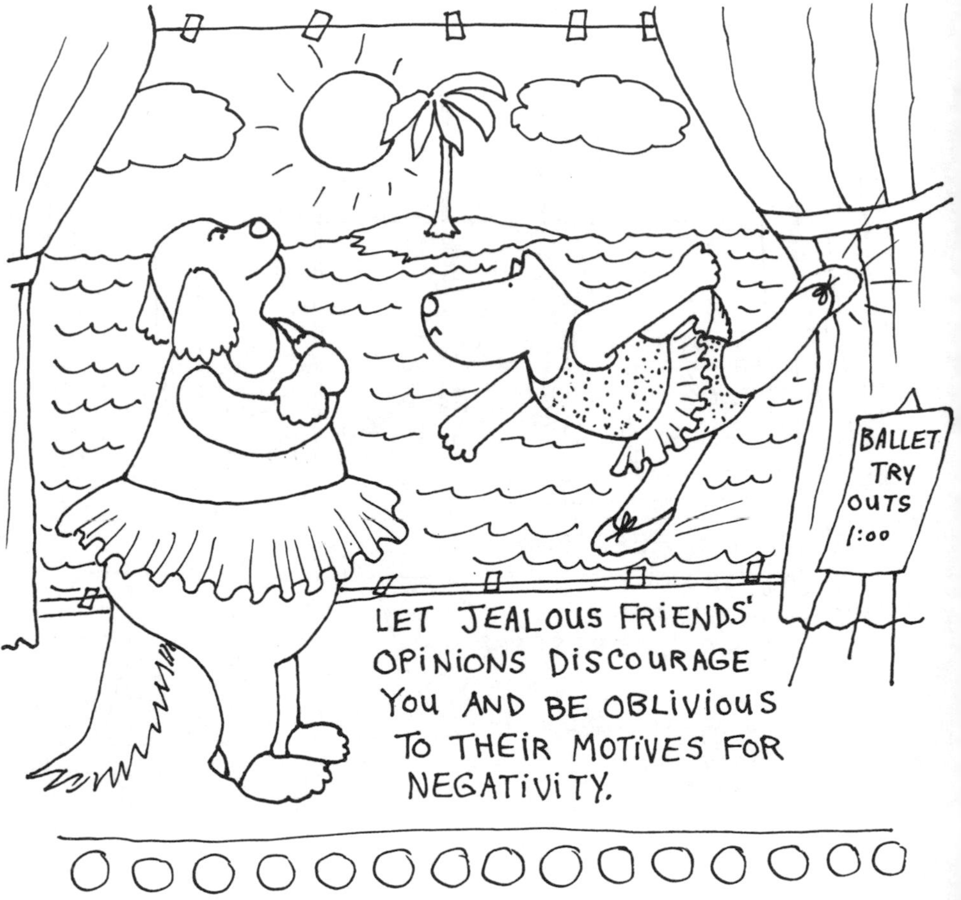
BALLET
TRY
OUTS
1:00
LET JEALOUS FRIENDS' OPINIONS DISCOURAGE YOU AND BE OBLIVIOUS TO THEIR MOTIVES FOR NEGATIVITY.

VOLUNTEER FOR YET ANOTHER COMMITTEE RATHER THAN TAKE YOUR SCULPTURE CLASS.

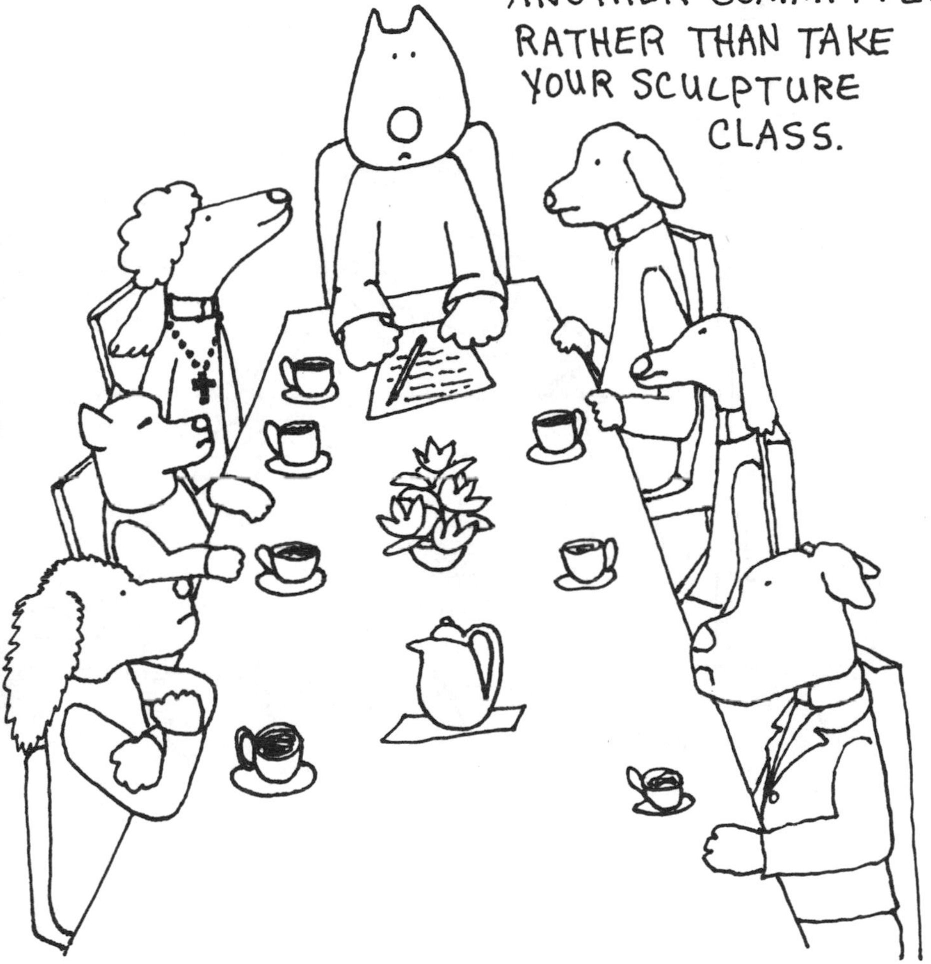

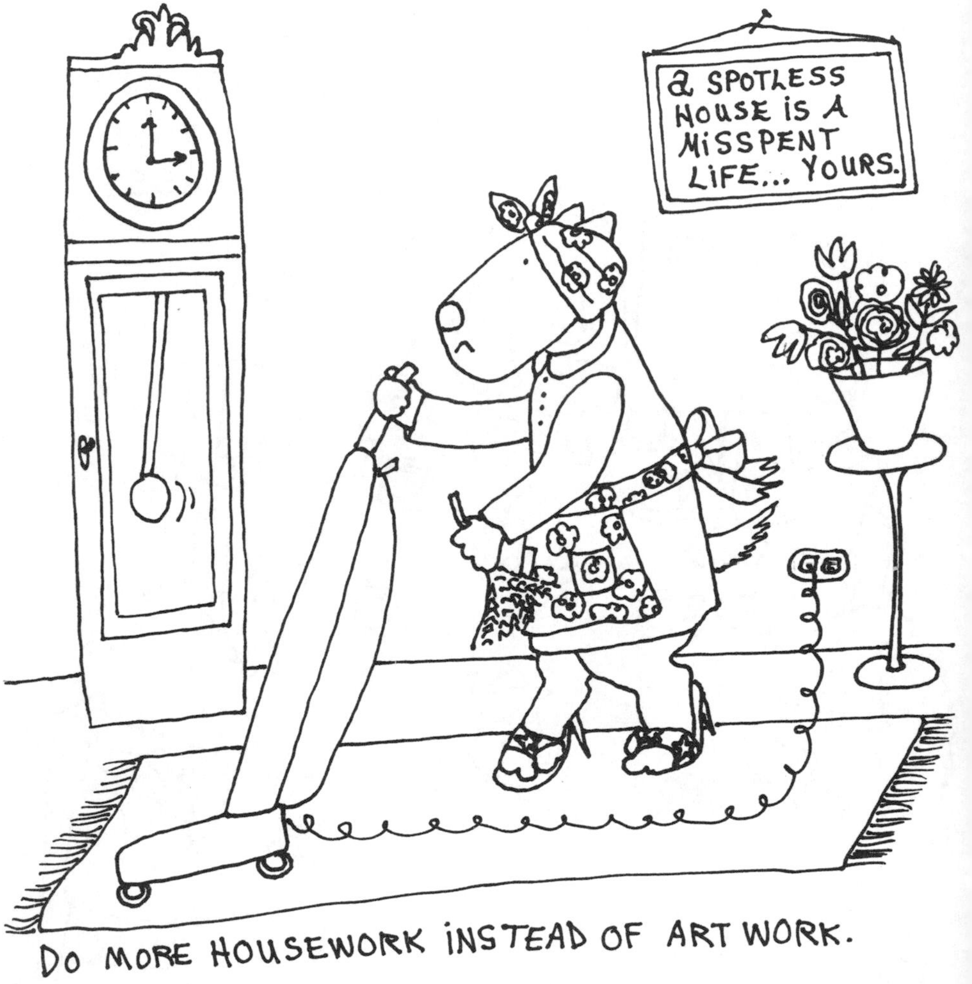
A SPOTLESS
HOUSE IS A
MISSPENT
LIFE... YOURS.

DO MORE HOUSEWORK INSTEAD OF ART WORK.

HELP YOUR TYRANNICAL
BOSS BURN HIS MIDNIGHT
OIL INSTEAD OF BURNING
YOURS. (LIKE MAYBE ON
YOUR ART!)

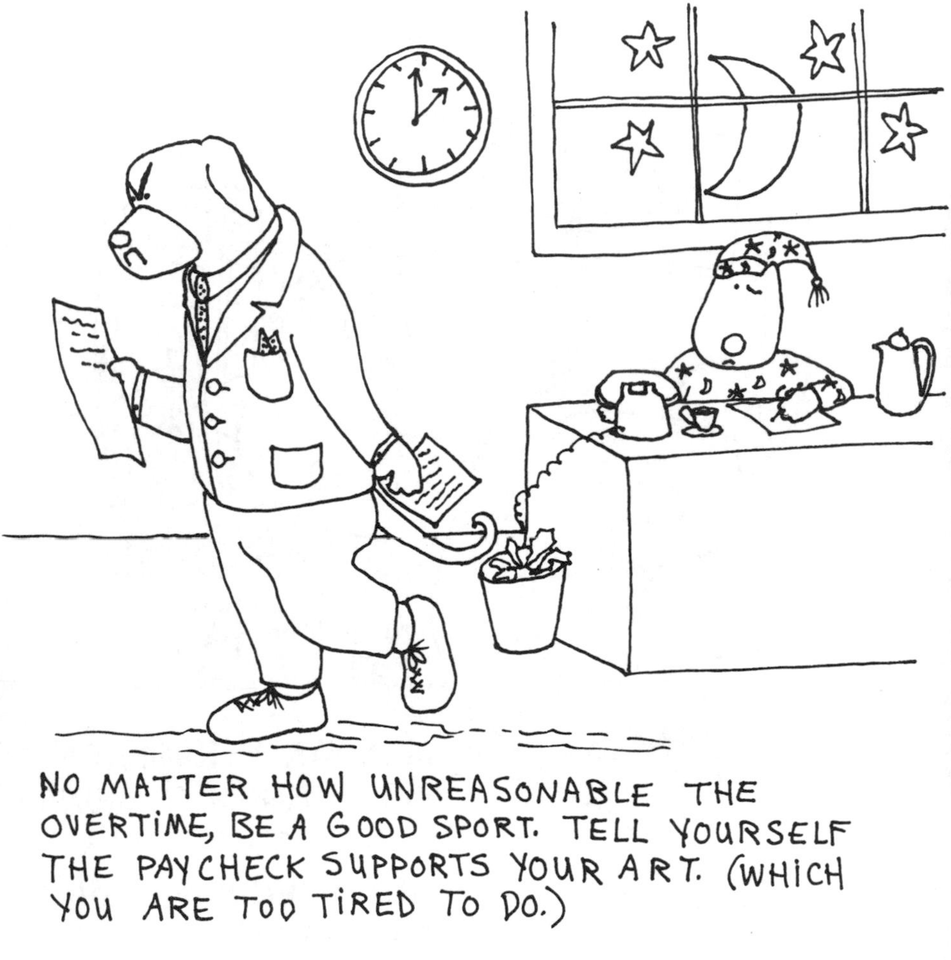

NO MATTER HOW UNREASONABLE THE OVERTIME, BE A GOOD SPORT. TELL YOURSELF THE PAYCHECK SUPPORTS YOUR ART. (WHICH YOU ARE TOO TIRED TO DO.)

INSTEAD OF LOOKING
FOR A NEW JOB
MOVE A SLEEPING
BAG INTO THE
OFFICE.

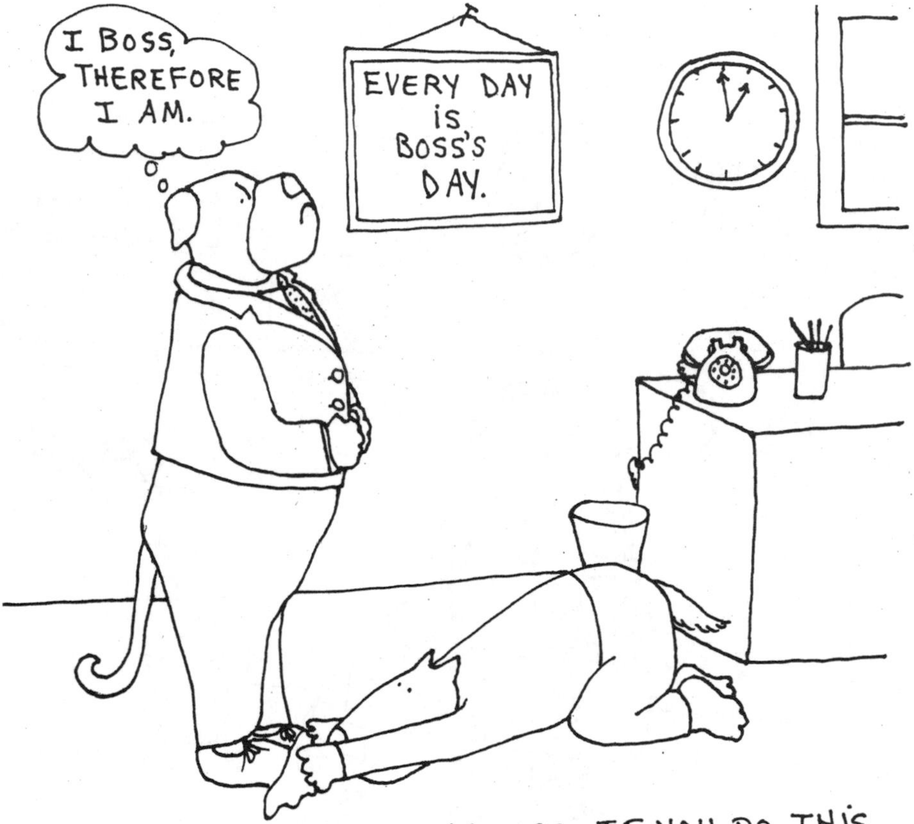
I BOSS, THEREFORE I AM.
EVERY DAY iS BOSS'S DAY.

POLISH HIS ALREADY BIG EGO. IF YOU DO THIS WELL ENOUGH, YOU'LL NEVER HAVE TIME FOR YOUR OWN WORK.

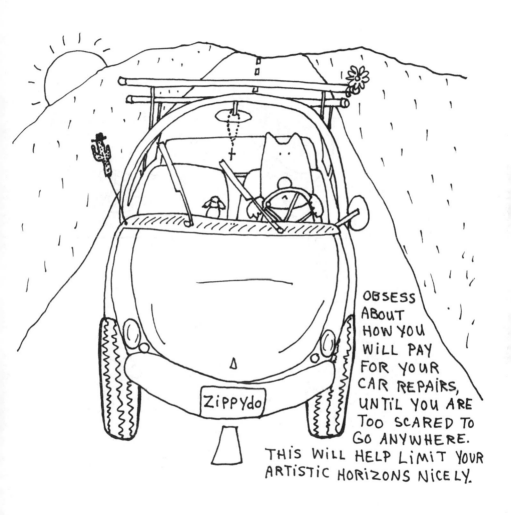

OBSESS ABOUT HOW YOU WILL PAY FOR YOUR CAR REPAIRS, UNTIL YOU ARE TOO SCARED TO GO ANYWHERE. THIS WILL HELP LIMIT YOUR ARTISTIC HORIZONS NICELY.

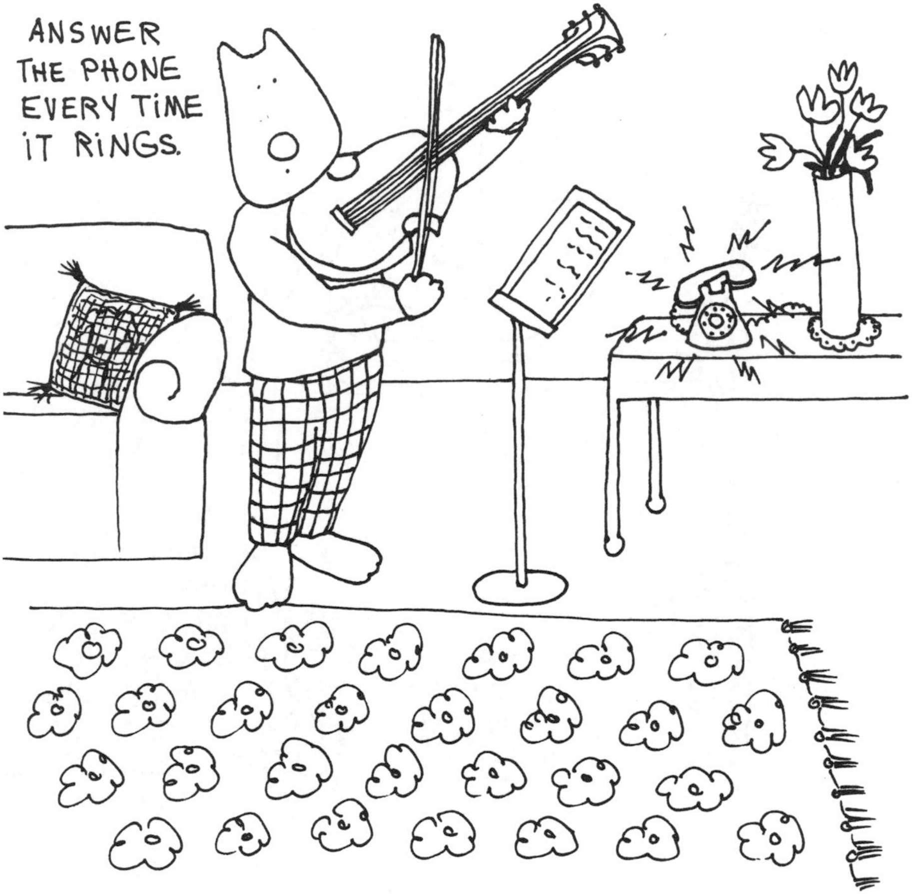
ANSWER THE PHONE EVERY TIME IT RINGS.

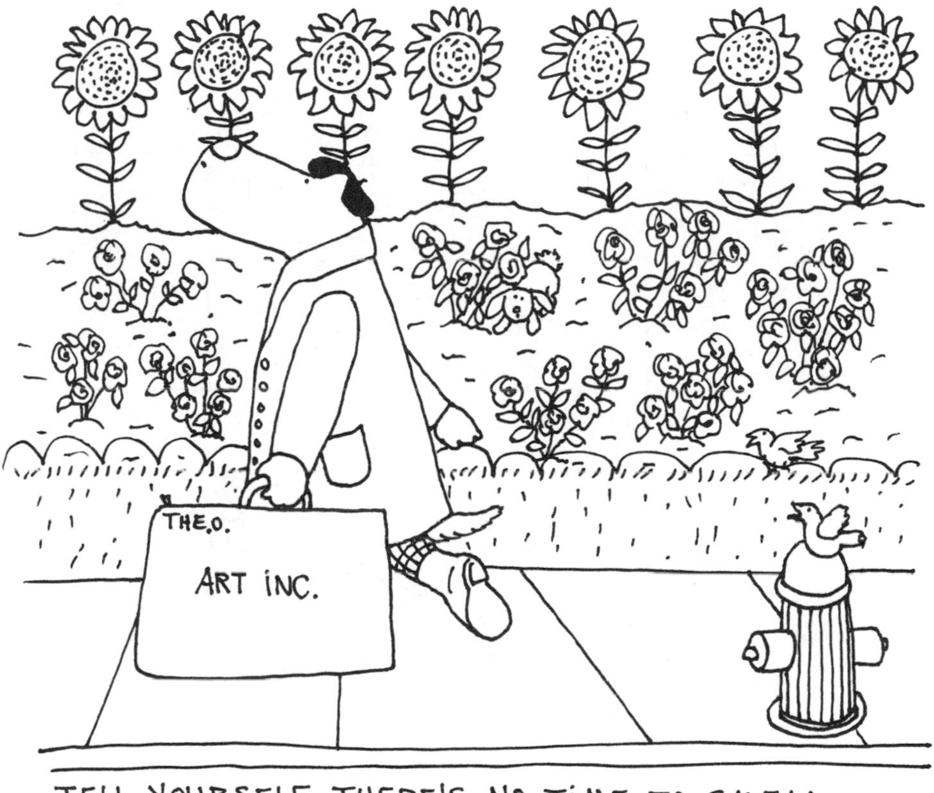
THE.O.
ART INC.

TELL YOURSELF THERE'S NO TIME TO SMELL THE ROSES, LET ALONE PAINT THEM.

CHOOSE COMPANIONS WHOSE
DEPRESSION IS CATCHING.

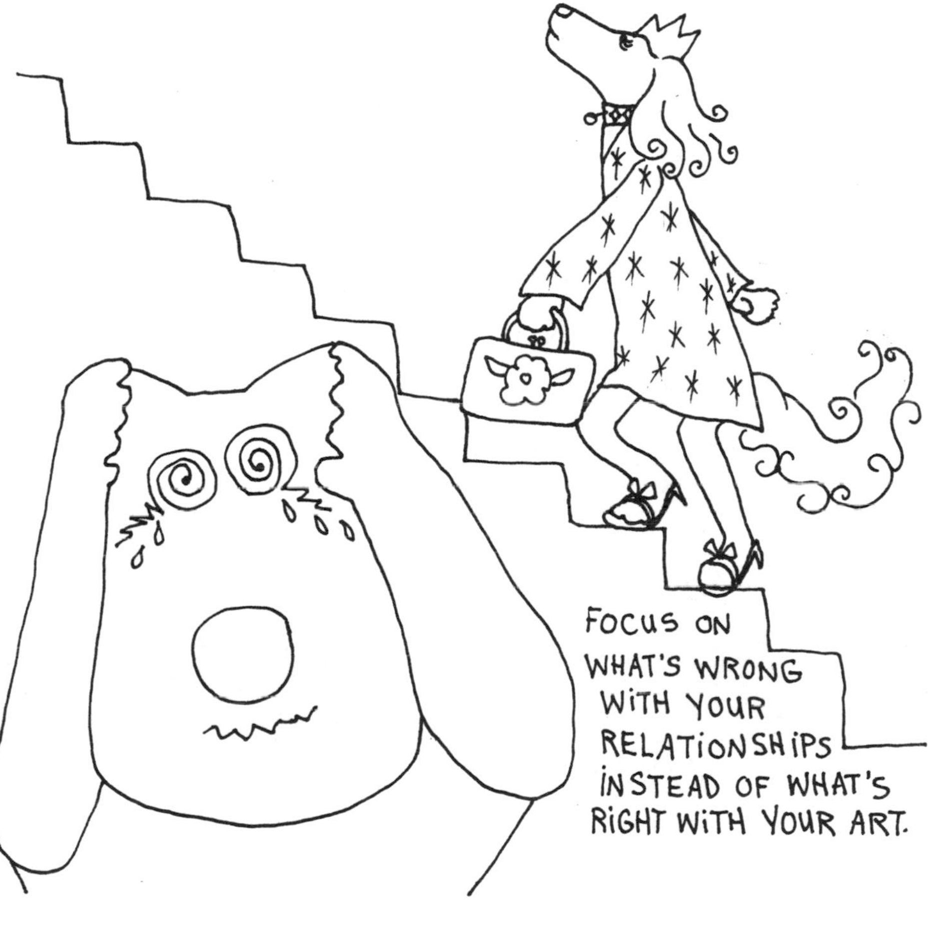
FOCUS ON
WHAT'S WRONG
WITH YOUR
RELATIONSHIPS
INSTEAD OF WHAT'S
RIGHT WITH YOUR ART.

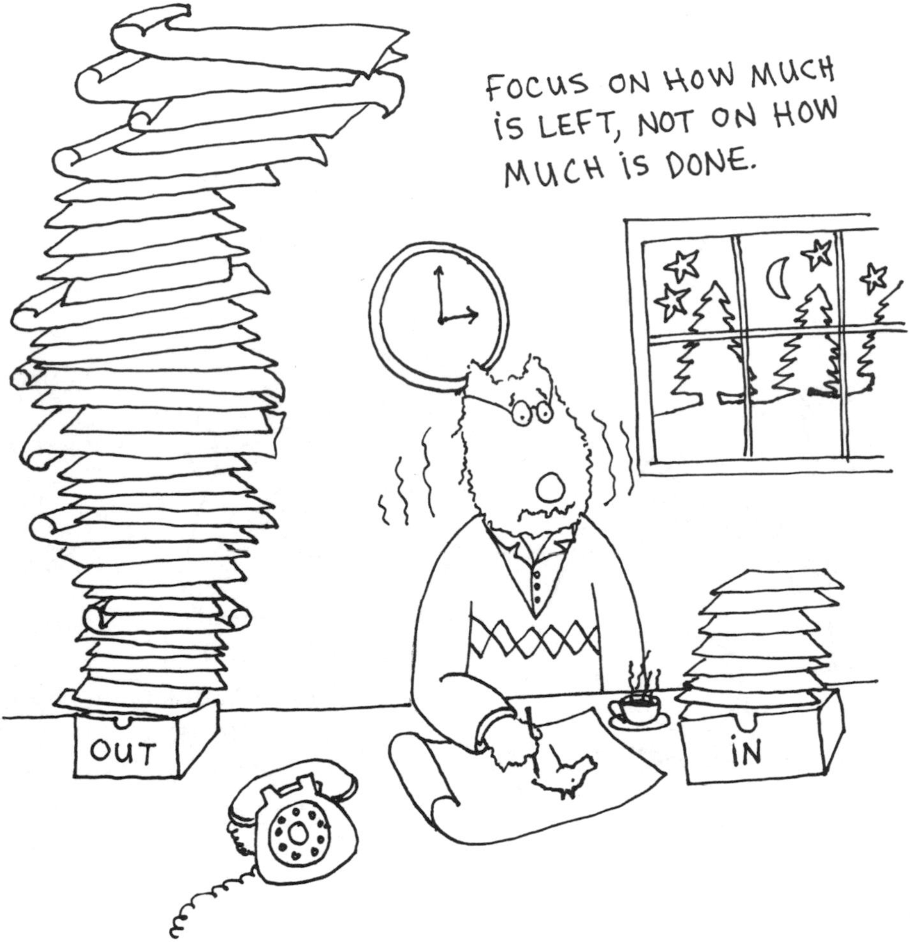
FOCUS ON HOW MUCH IS LEFT, NOT ON HOW MUCH IS DONE.
OUT
IN

UNDER NO CIRCUMSTANCES
MAKE ANY ART JUST FOR FUN.

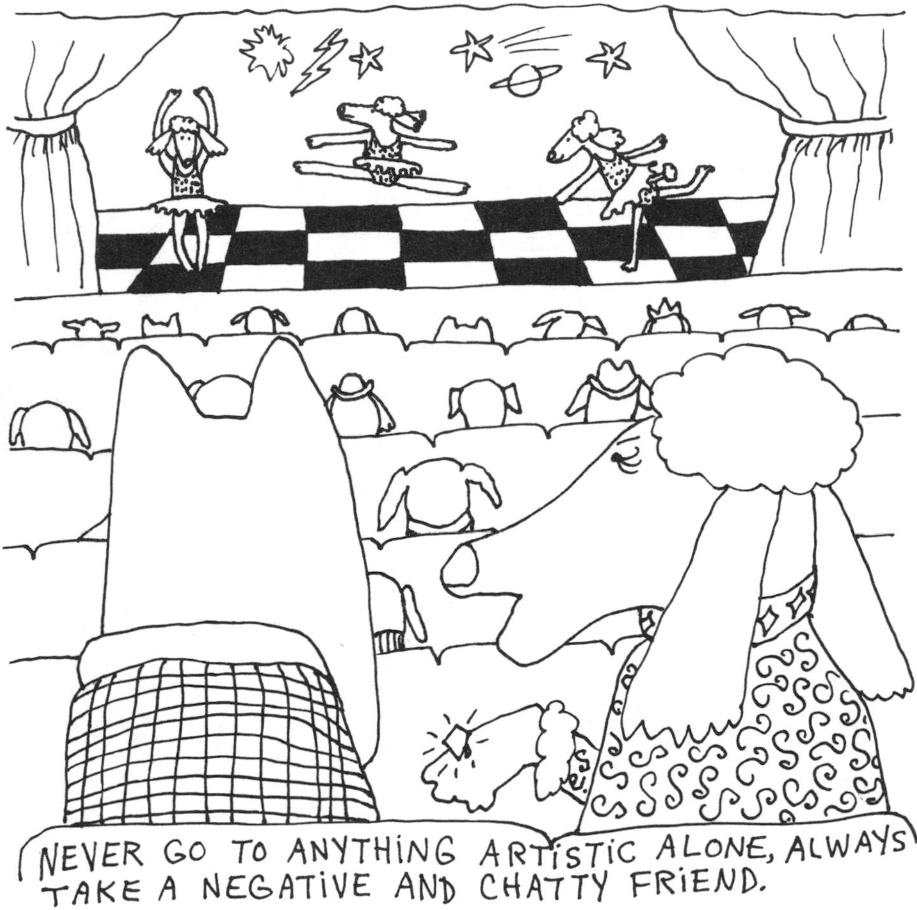

NEVER GO TO ANYTHING ARTISTIC ALONE, ALWAYS TAKE A NEGATIVE AND CHATTY FRIEND.

CONCENTRATE ON HOW YOU WANT YOUR "BIG BREAK," AND IGNORE ALL SMALLER ONES.

TELL YOURSELF YOU HAVE "NO TIME" FOR A HOBBY, THEN WATCH T.V. TO KEEP FROM BEING DEPRESSED.

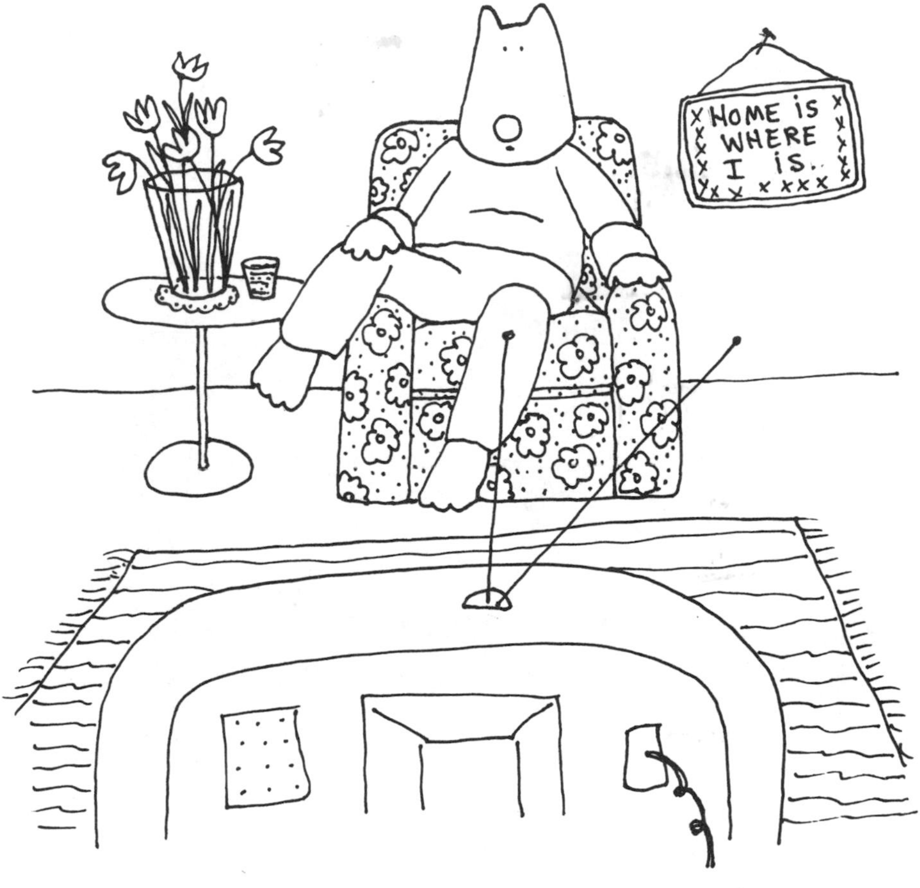
HOME IS WHERE I IS.

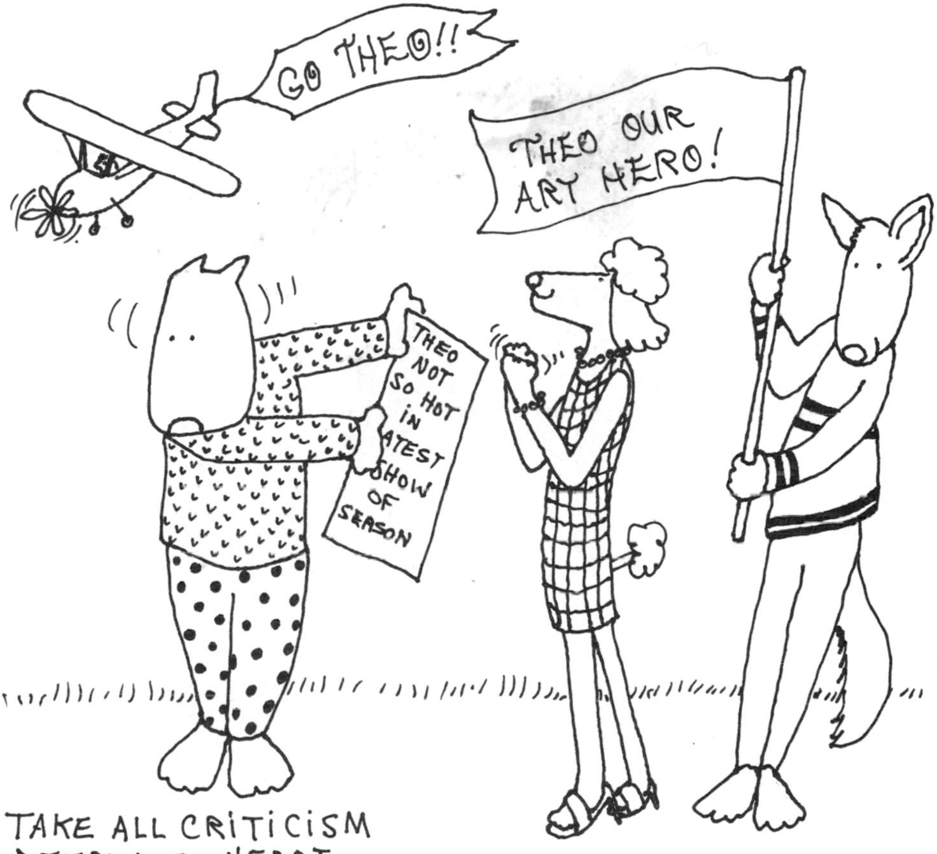
GO THEO!!
THEO OUR ART HERO!
THEO NOT SO HOT IN LATEST SHOW OF SEASON

TAKE ALL CRITICISM
DEEPLY TO HEART.
DISCOUNT ALL PRAISE.

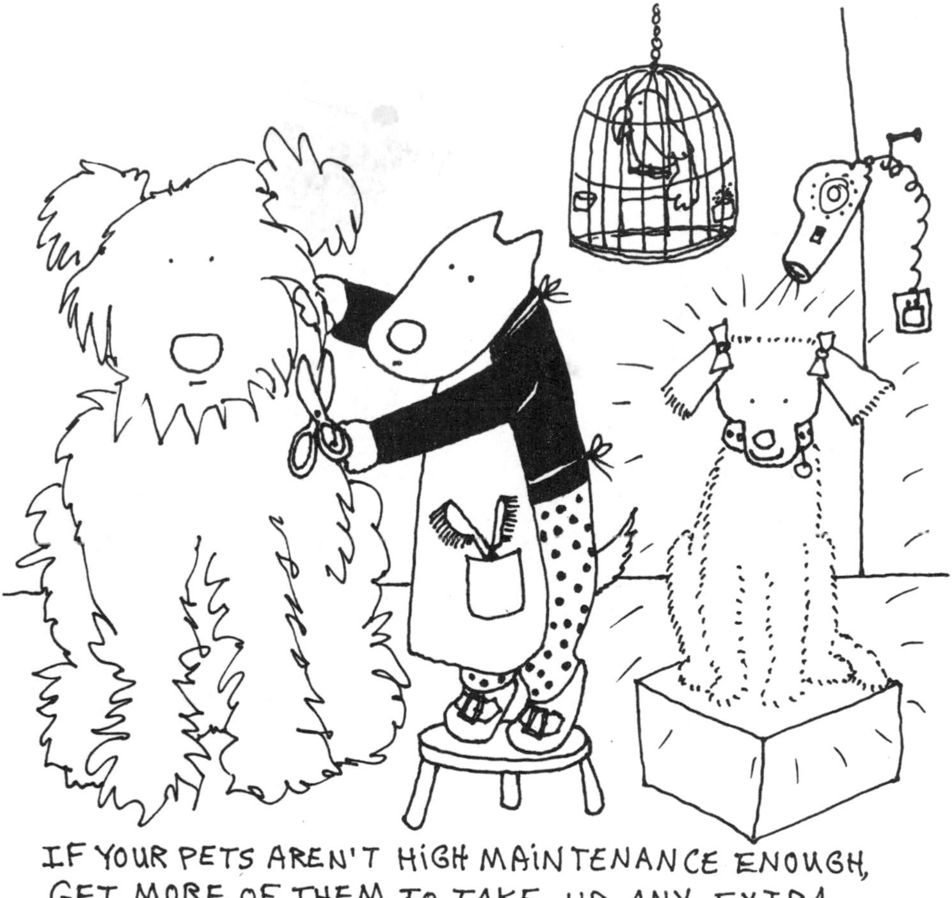

IF YOUR PETS AREN'T HIGH MAINTENANCE ENOUGH, GET MORE OF THEM TO TAKE UP ANY EXTRA FREE TIME OR MONEY YOU MIGHT HAVE.

MENTALLY READ THE BAD REVIEWS YOU WILL GET.

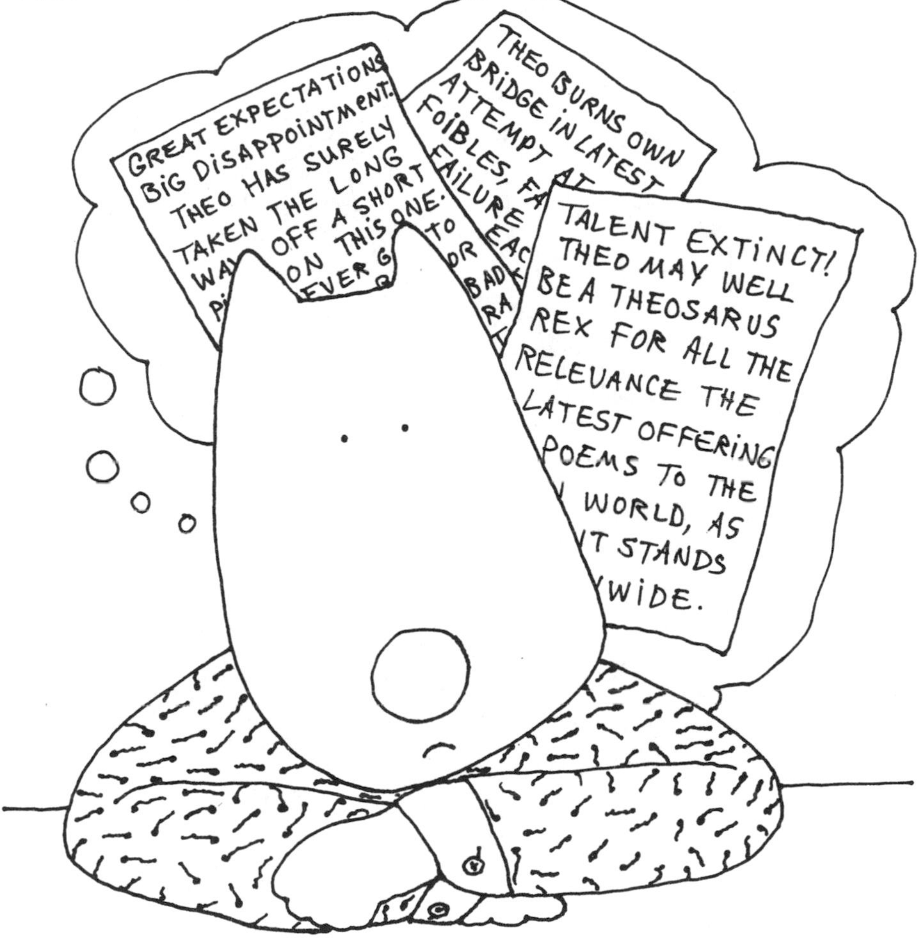
GREAT EXPECTATIONS BIG DISAPPOINTMENT. THEO HAS SURELY TAKEN THE LONG WAY OFF A SHORT ON THIS ONE. EVER
THEO BURNS OWN BRIDGE IN LATEST ATTEMPT FOIBLES, FAILURE TO OR BAD RA
TALENT EXTINCT! THEO MAY WELL BE A THEOSARUS REX FOR ALL THE RELEVANCE THE LATEST OFFERING POEMS TO THE WORLD, AS IT STANDS WIDE.

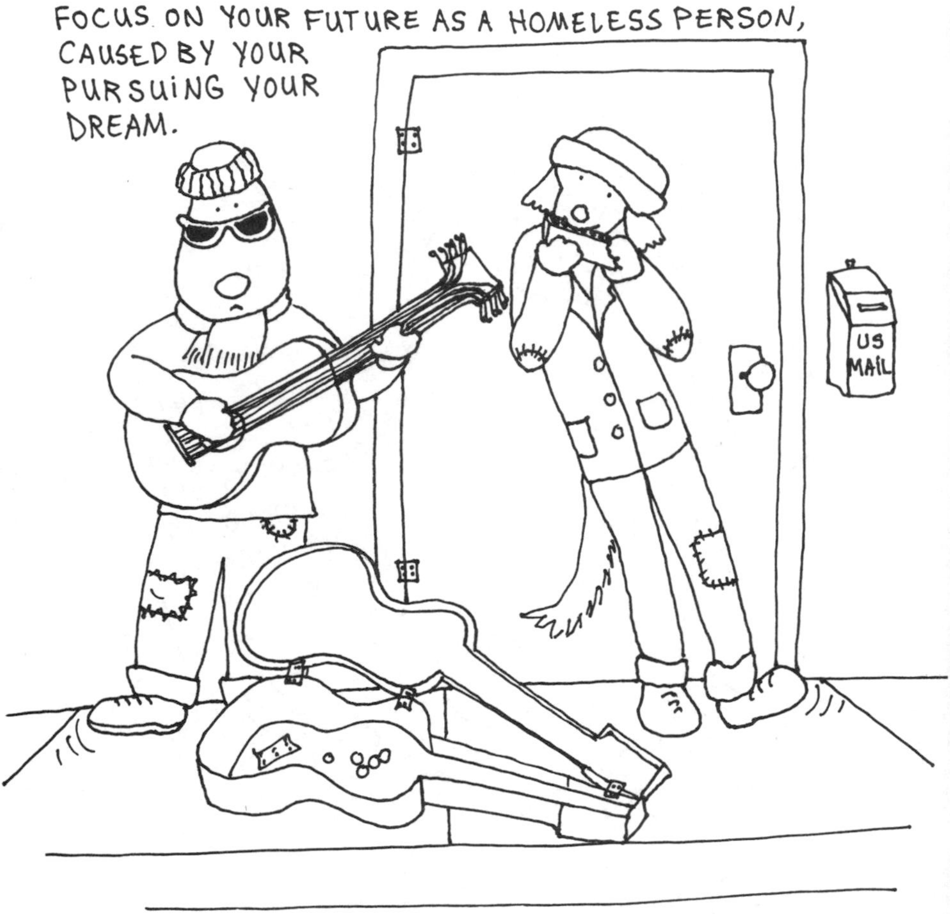
FOCUS ON YOUR FUTURE AS A HOMELESS PERSON, CAUSED BY YOUR PURSUING YOUR DREAM.
US MAIL

PRACTICE SAYING NO TO ANY AND ALL PLAYFUL SUGGESTIONS.

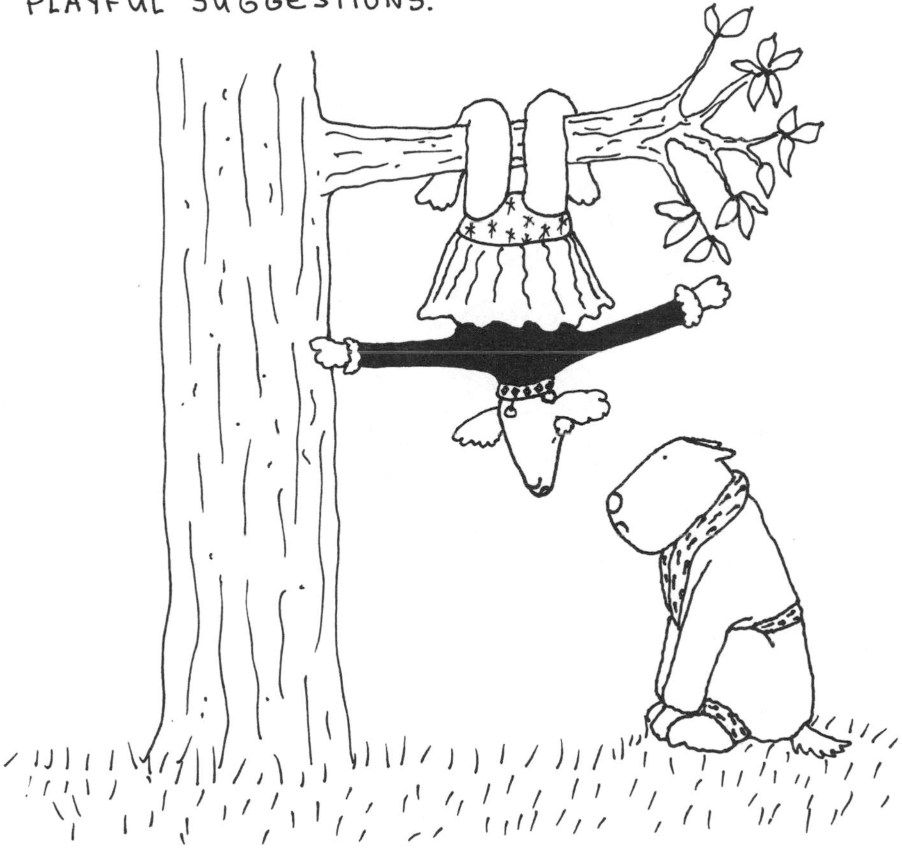

NEVER VENTURE INTO NEW ARTISTIC TERRITORY, NO MATTER HOW TEMPTING.

TELL YOURSELF YOU CAN NO LONGER BE CREATIVE IN YOUR HOME TOWN.

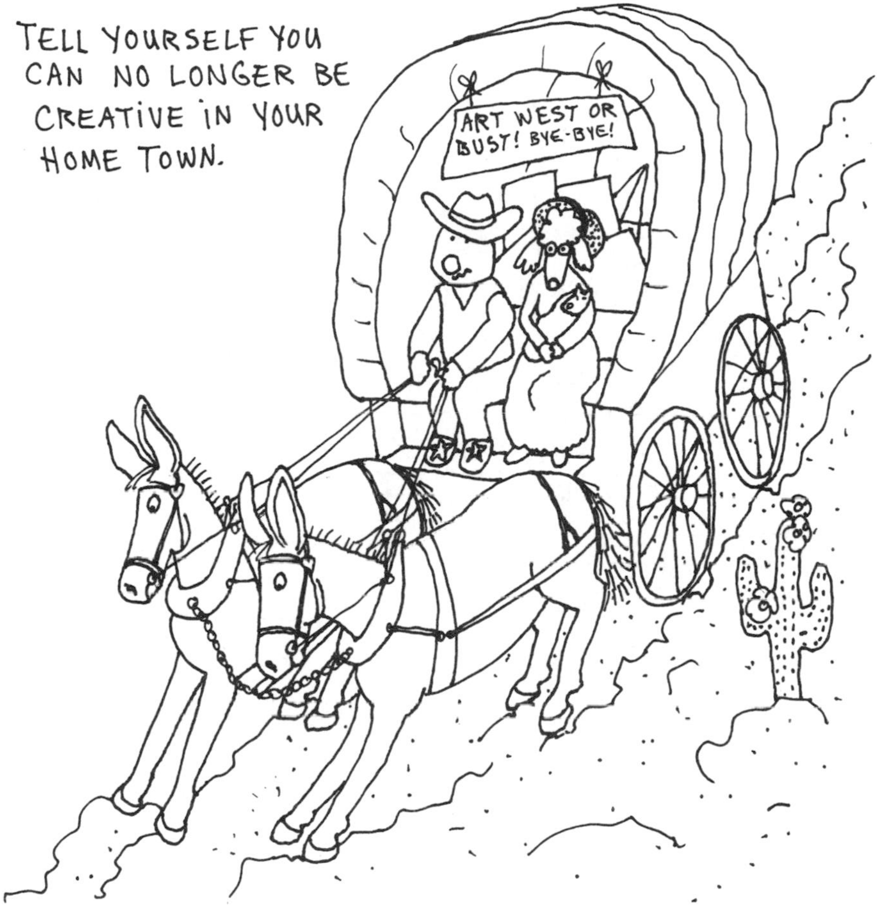
ART WEST OR BUST! BYE-BYE!

TELL YOURSELF YOU CAN'T AFFORD ART SUPPLIES.
BUY FIVE EXPENSIVE CAPPUCCINOS WHILE YOU
DISCUSS THIS WITH FRIENDS.

TELL YOURSELF YOU NEED TO RELAX INSTEAD OF
CREATE. TELL YOURSELF YOU'LL WRITE LATER.

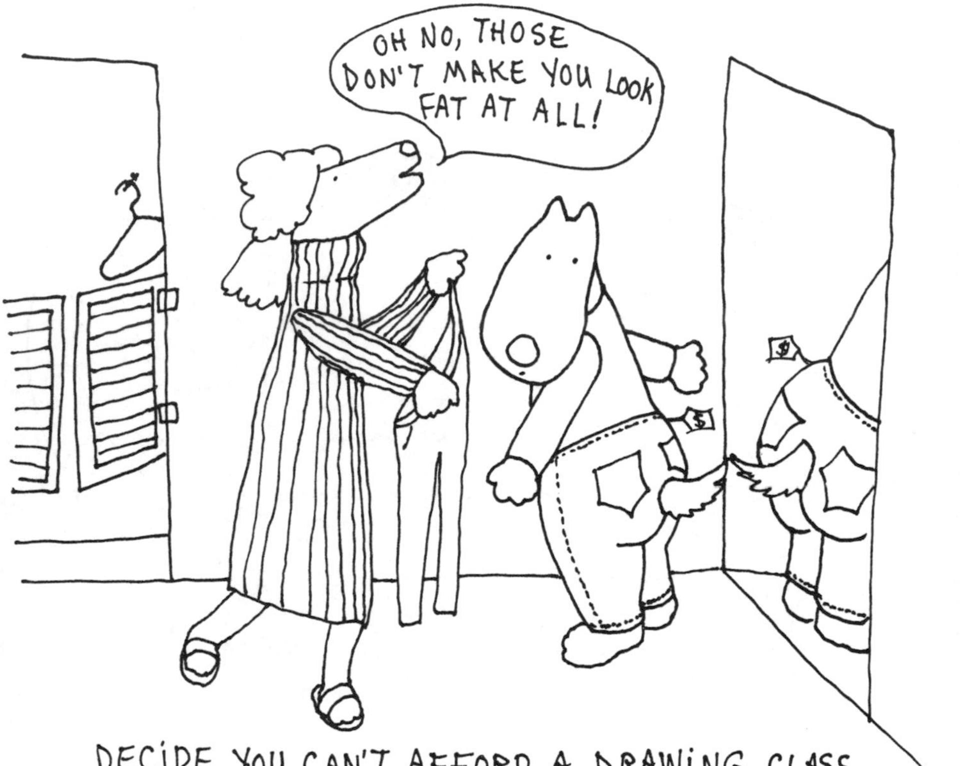
OH NO, THOSE DON'T MAKE YOU LOOK FAT AT ALL!

DECIDE YOU CAN'T AFFORD A DRAWING CLASS AND GET NEW JEANS TO CONSOLE YOURSELF.

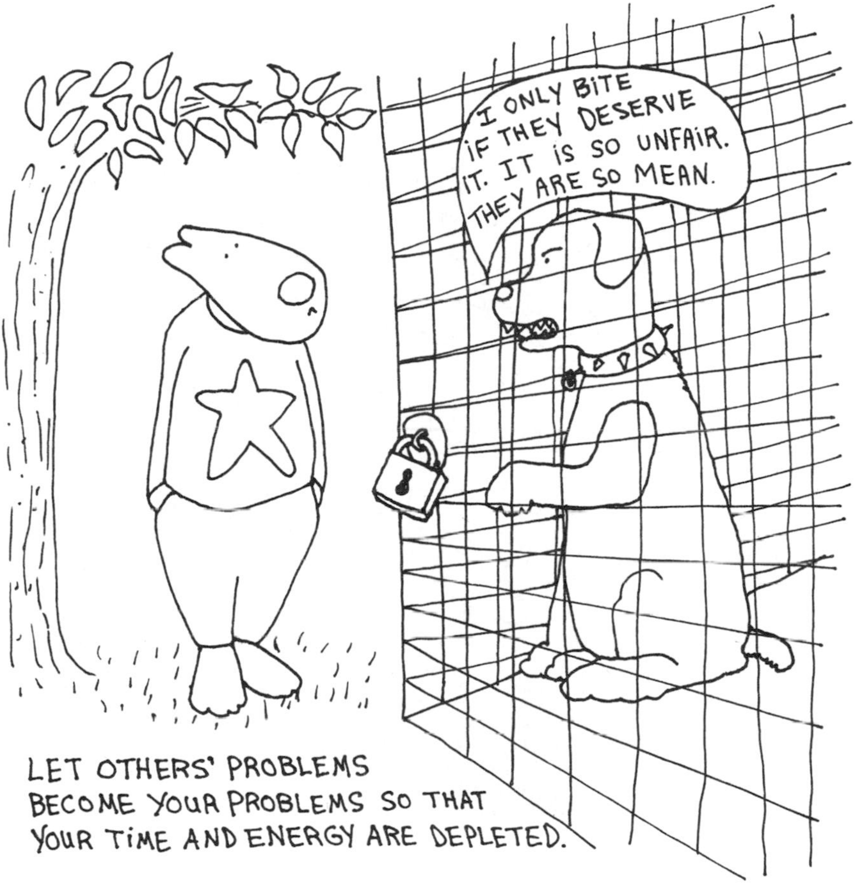
I ONLY BITE IF THEY DESERVE IT. IT IS SO UNFAIR. THEY ARE SO MEAN.

LET OTHERS' PROBLEMS
BECOME YOUR PROBLEMS SO THAT
YOUR TIME AND ENERGY ARE DEPLETED.

GET YOUR MAIN SENSE OF SELF WORTH HELPING OTHERS INSTEAD OF FACING THE BLANK PAGE.

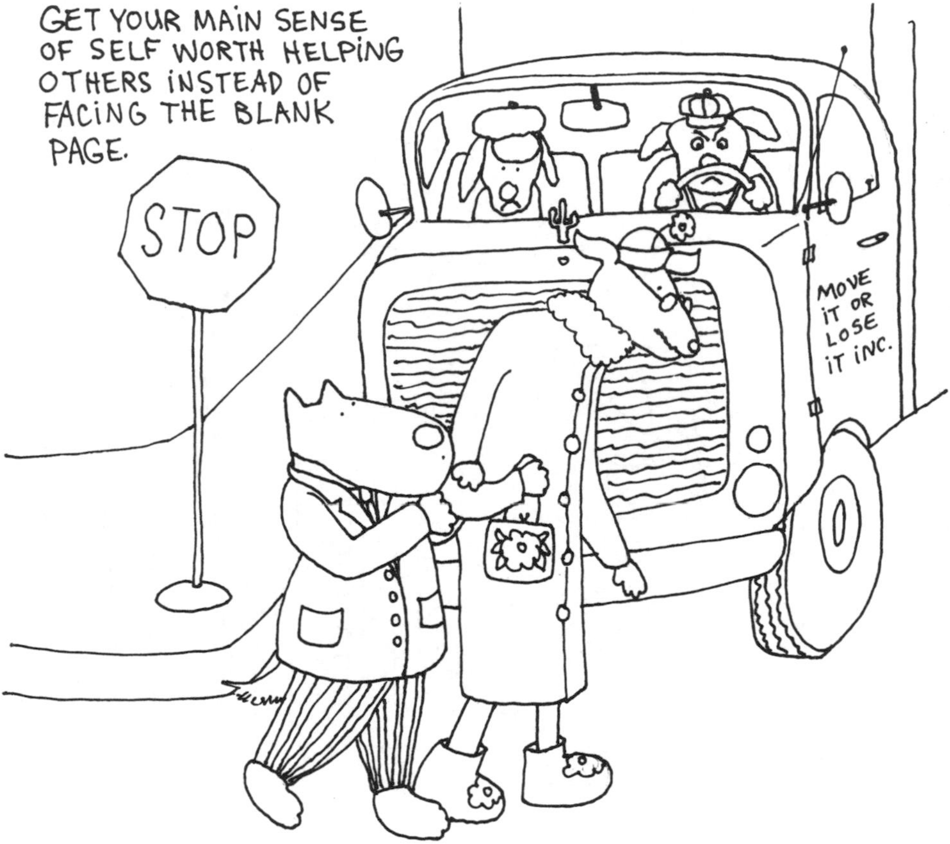
STOP
MOVE IT OR LOSE IT INC.

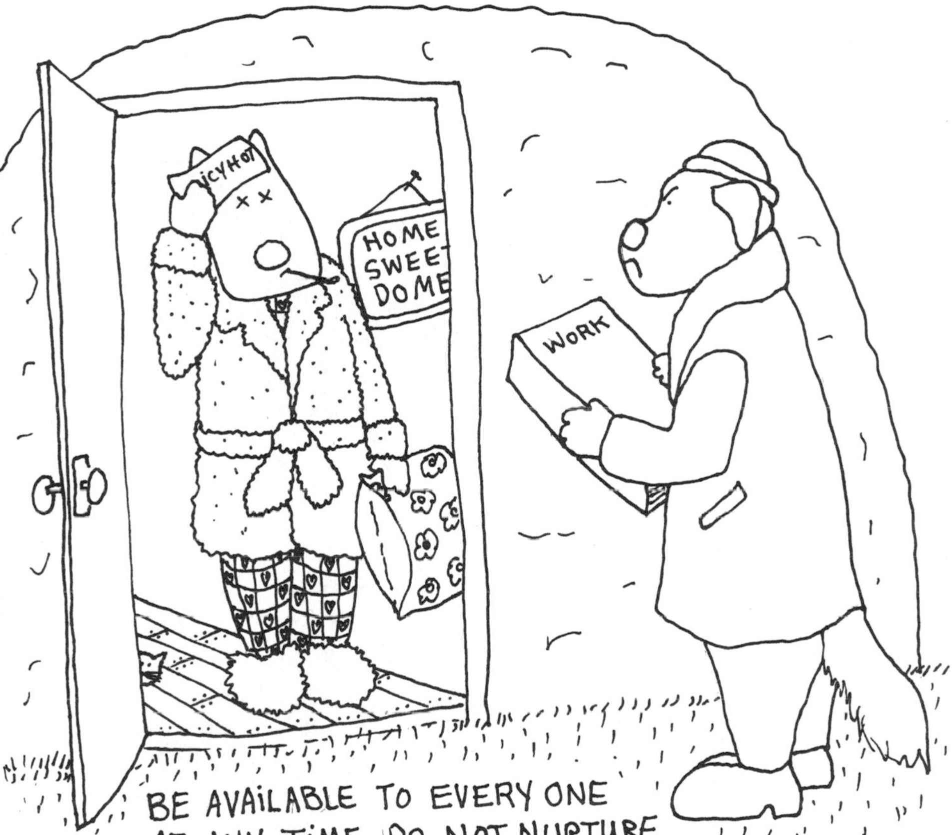
ICYHOT
HOME
SWEET
DOME
WORK

BE AVAILABLE TO EVERY ONE AT ANY TIME. DO NOT NURTURE YOURSELF OR SET BOUNDARIES.

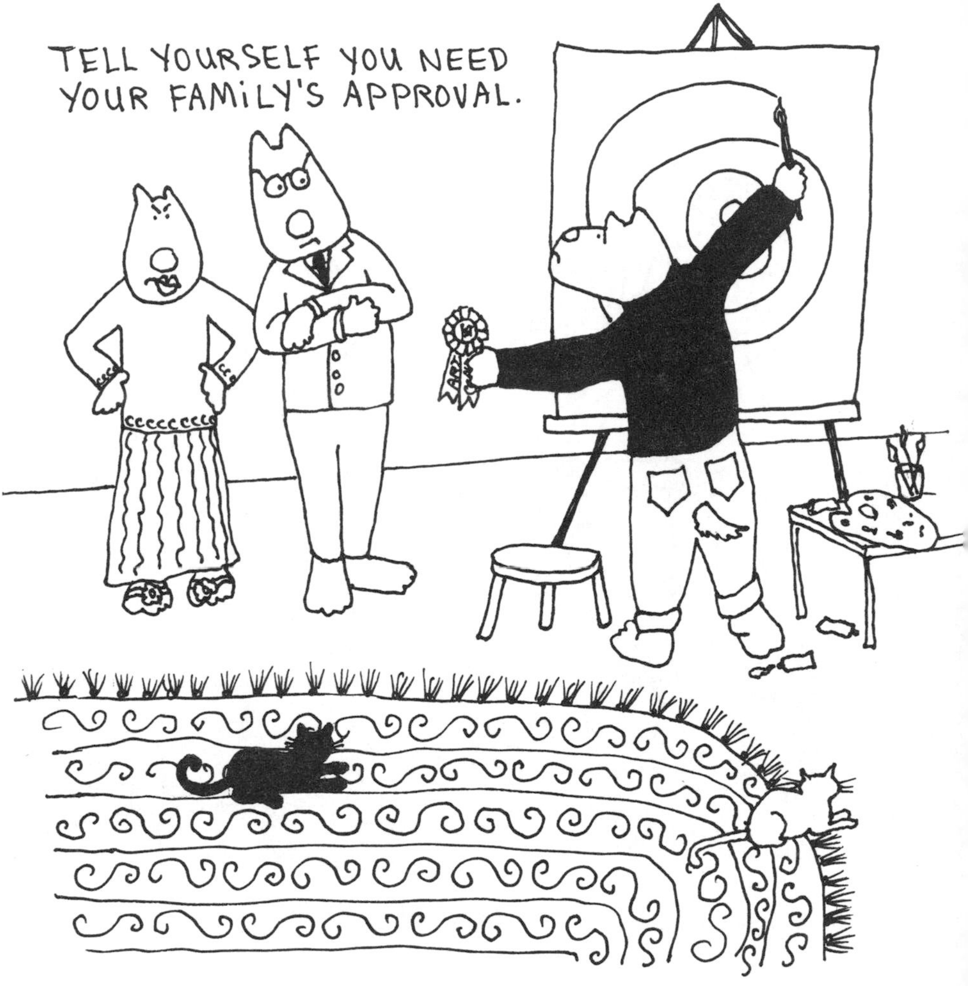
TELL YOURSELF YOU NEED YOUR FAMILY'S APPROVAL.

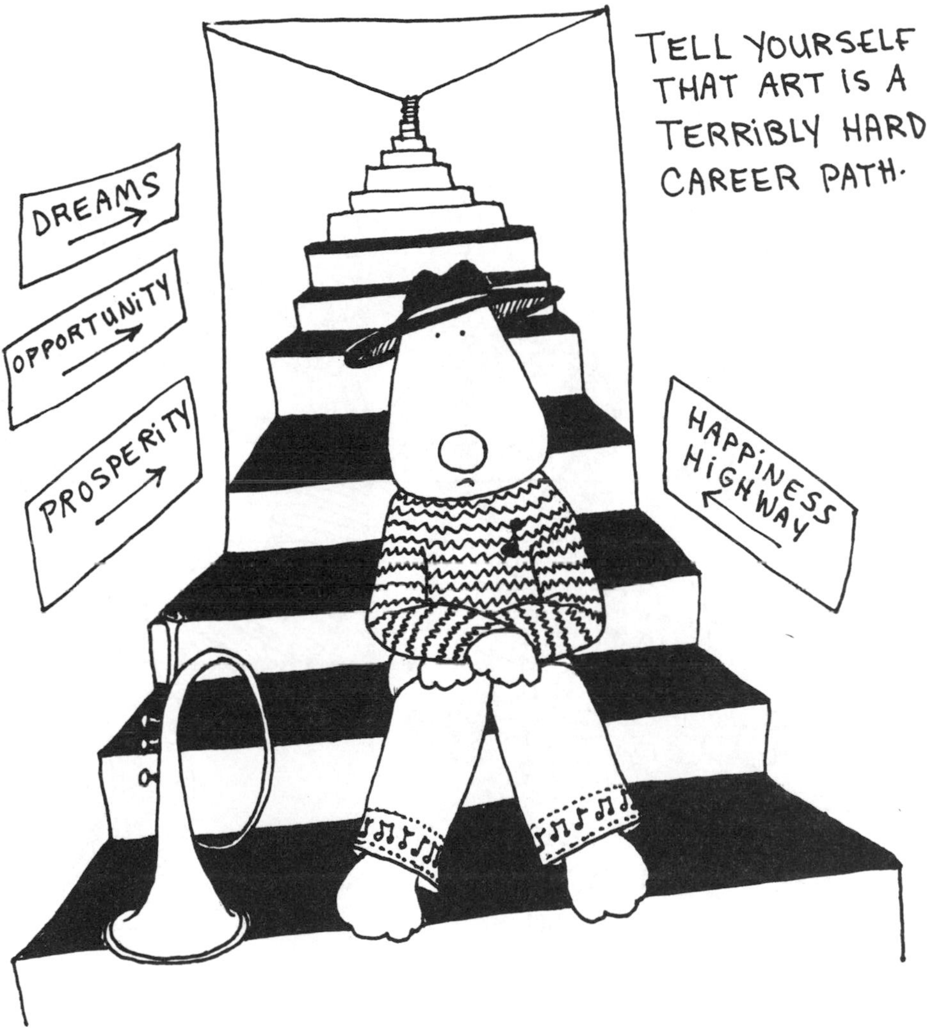
TELL YOURSELF THAT ART IS A TERRIBLY HARD CAREER PATH.
DREAMS
OPPORTUNITY
PROSPERITY
HAPPINESS HIGHWAY

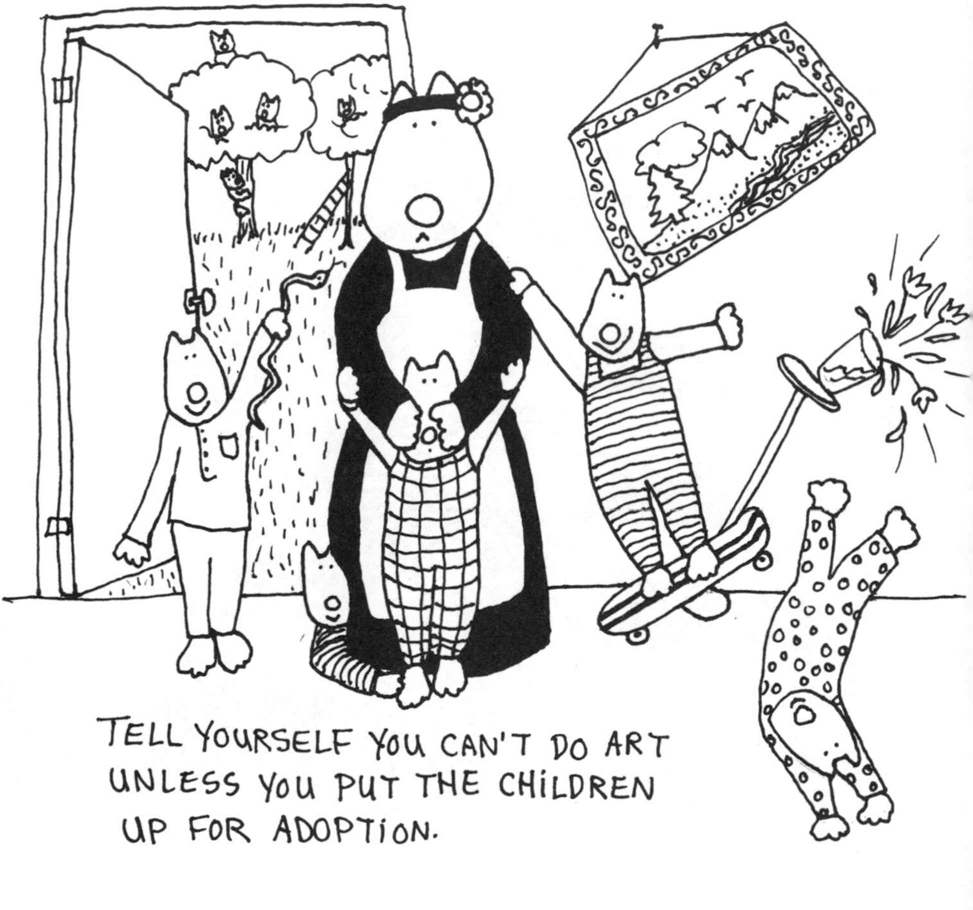

TELL YOURSELF YOU CAN'T DO ART UNLESS YOU PUT THE CHILDREN UP FOR ADOPTION.

TELL YOURSELF YOU'LL LOOK RIDICULOUS
TO YOUNG FANS OF YOUR ART FORM.

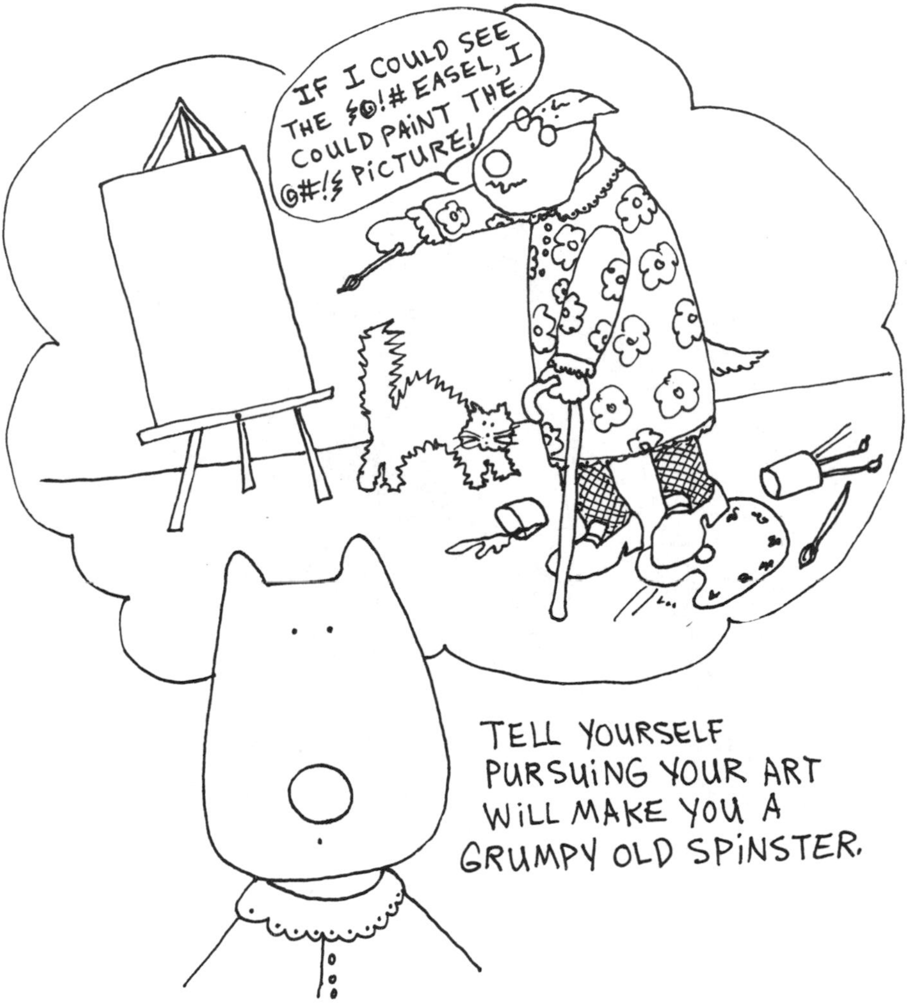
IF I COULD SEE THE $@!# EASEL, I COULD PAINT THE @#!$ PICTURE!

TELL YOURSELF PURSUING YOUR ART WILL MAKE YOU A GRUMPY OLD SPINSTER.

TELL YOURSELF YOU DON'T WANT TO GET TYPE-
CAST AND THEN TURN DOWN THAT ACTING JOB.

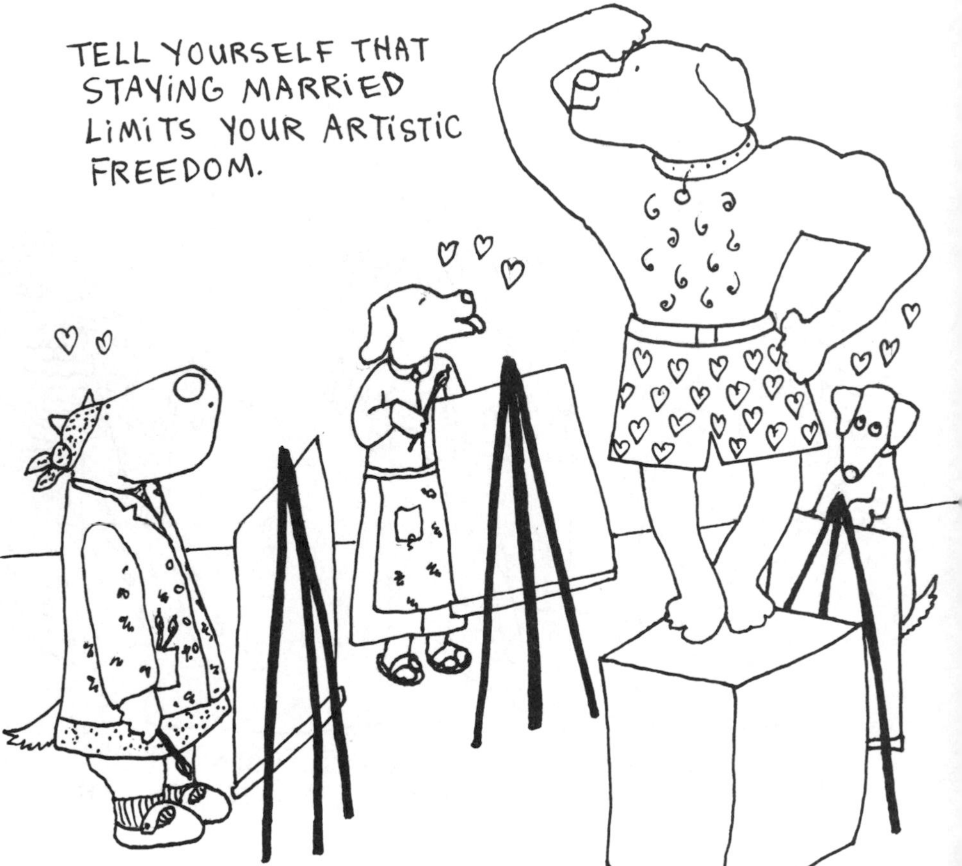
TELL YOURSELF THAT STAYING MARRIED LIMITS YOUR ARTISTIC FREEDOM.

TELL YOURSELF YOUR WORK ISN'T GOOD ENOUGH TO FINISH OR FRAME. EXPLAIN TO EVERYONE THAT YOU'RE NOT "REALLY" AN ARTIST...

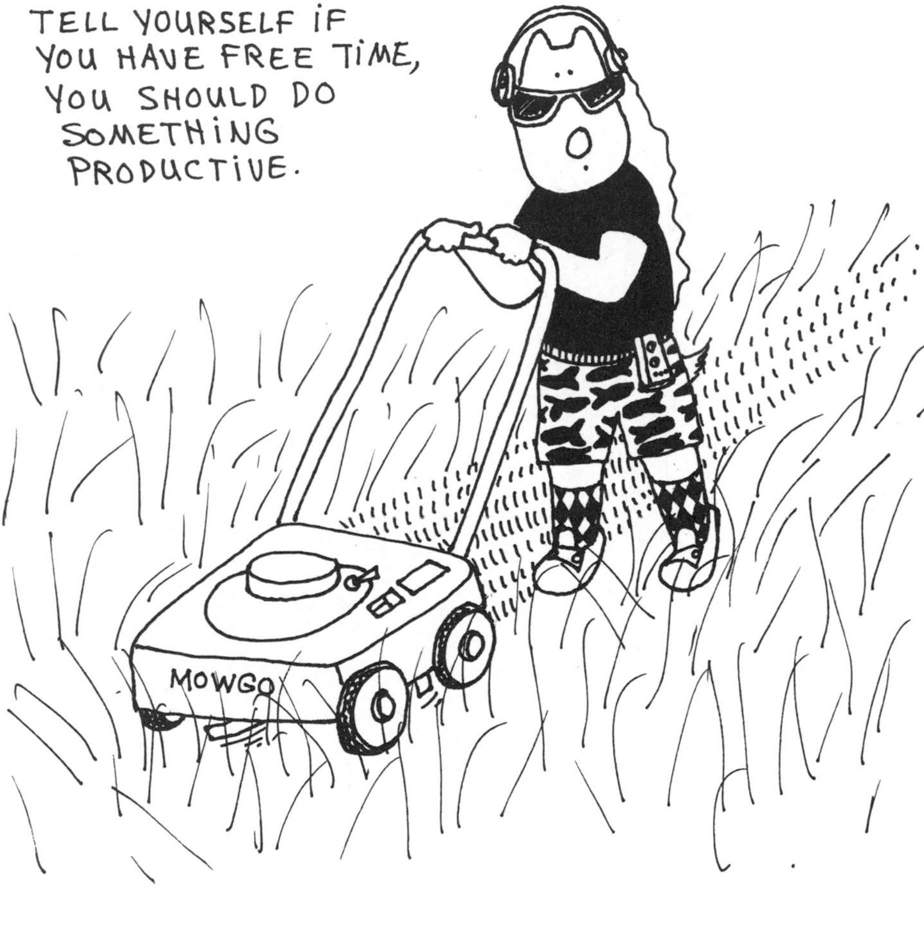
TELL YOURSELF IF YOU HAVE FREE TIME, YOU SHOULD DO SOMETHING PRODUCTIVE.
MOWGO

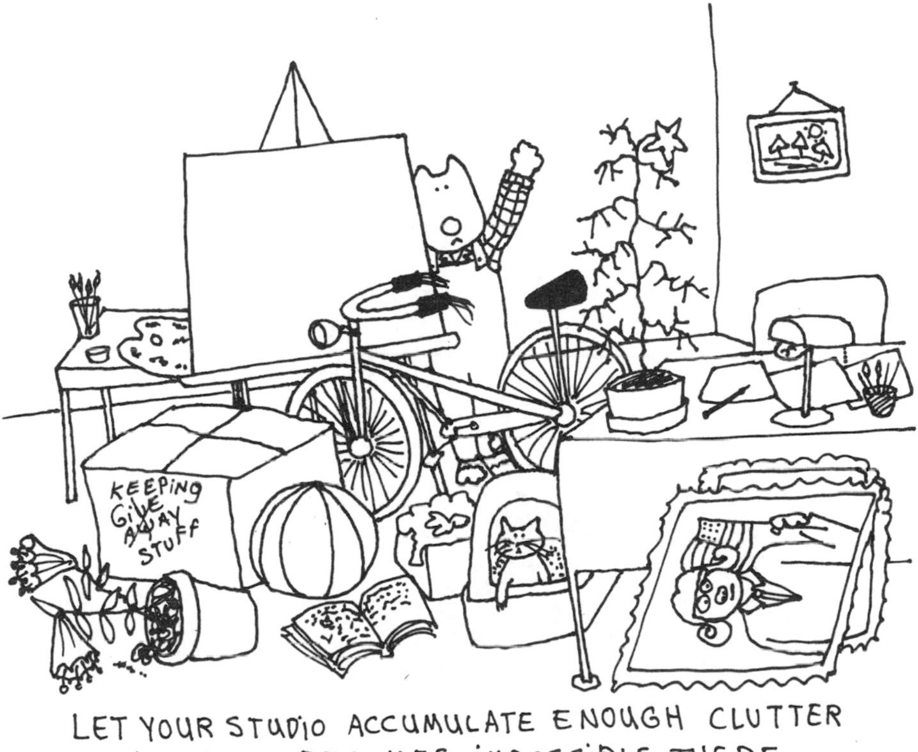
KEEPING
GIVE AWAY
STUFF

LET YOUR STUDIO ACCUMULATE ENOUGH CLUTTER THAT WORK BECOMES IMPOSSIBLE THERE.

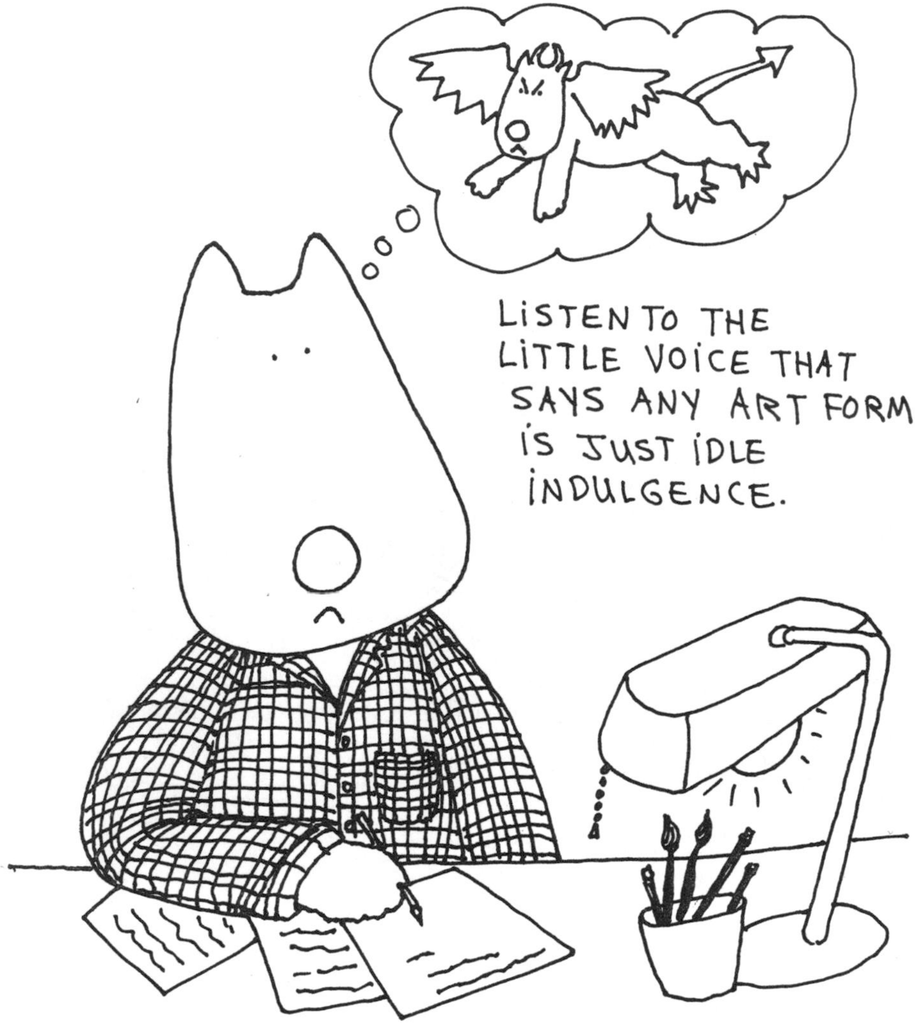
LISTEN TO THE LITTLE VOICE THAT SAYS ANY ART FORM IS JUST IDLE INDULGENCE.

SEEK OUT A DISILLUSIONED ELDER STATESMAN FOR YOUR MENTOR.

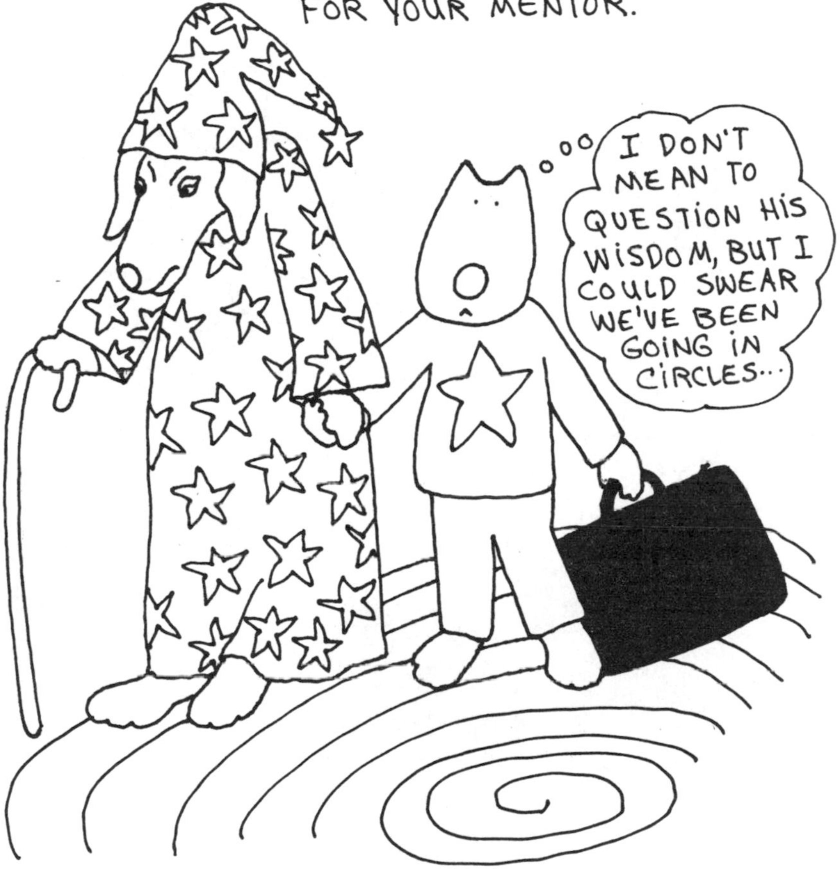
I DON'T MEAN TO QUESTION HIS WISDOM, BUT I COULD SWEAR WE'VE BEEN GOING IN CIRCLES...

ASK A LOT OF PEOPLE THEIR OPINION OF YOUR PLAN.

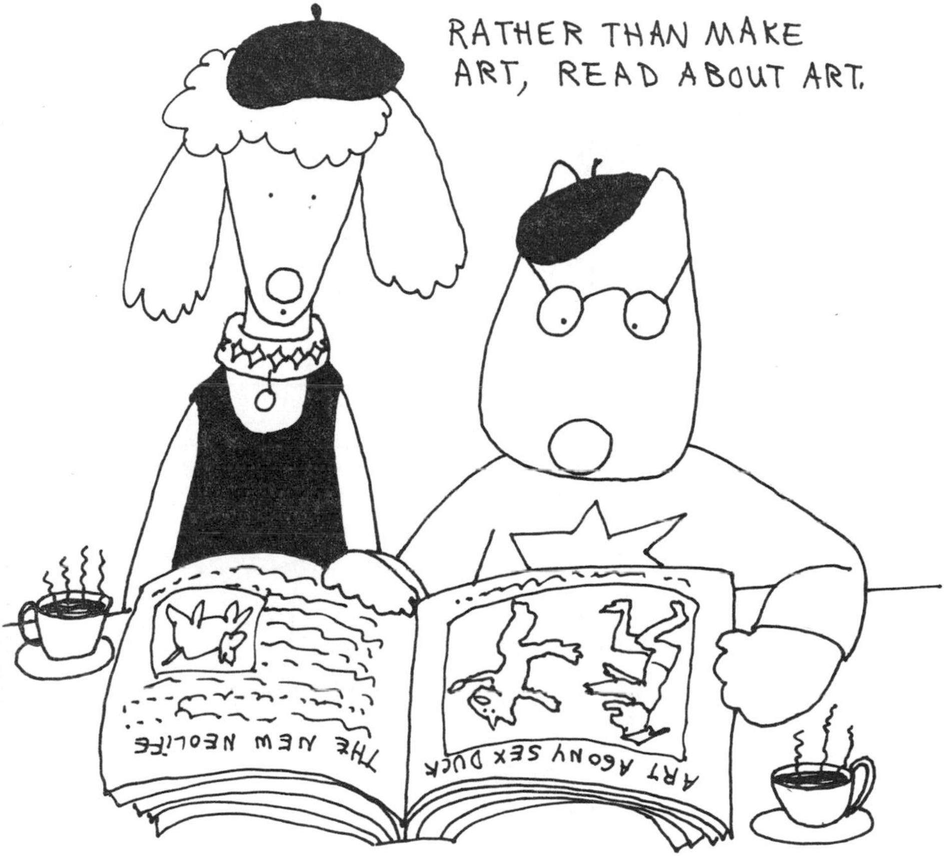
RATHER THAN MAKE ART, READ ABOUT ART.
THE NEW NEOLIFE
ART AGONY SEX DUCK

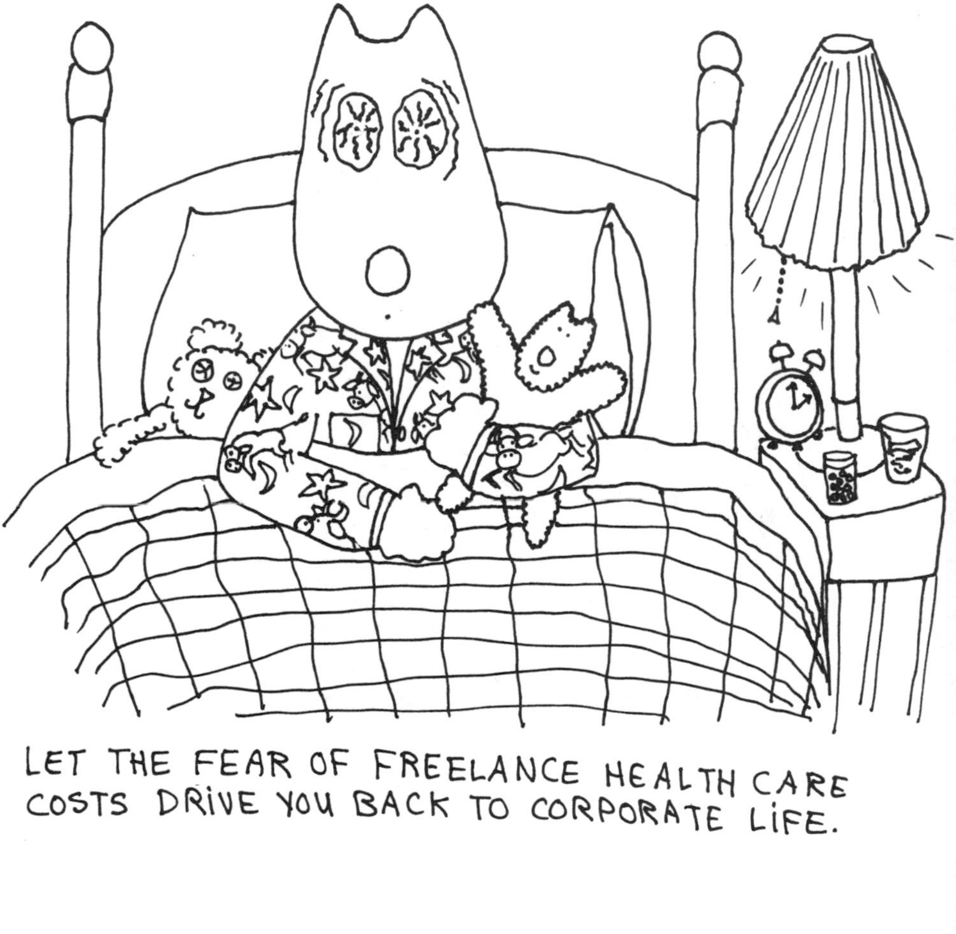

LET THE FEAR OF FREELANCE HEALTH CARE COSTS DRIVE YOU BACK TO CORPORATE LIFE.

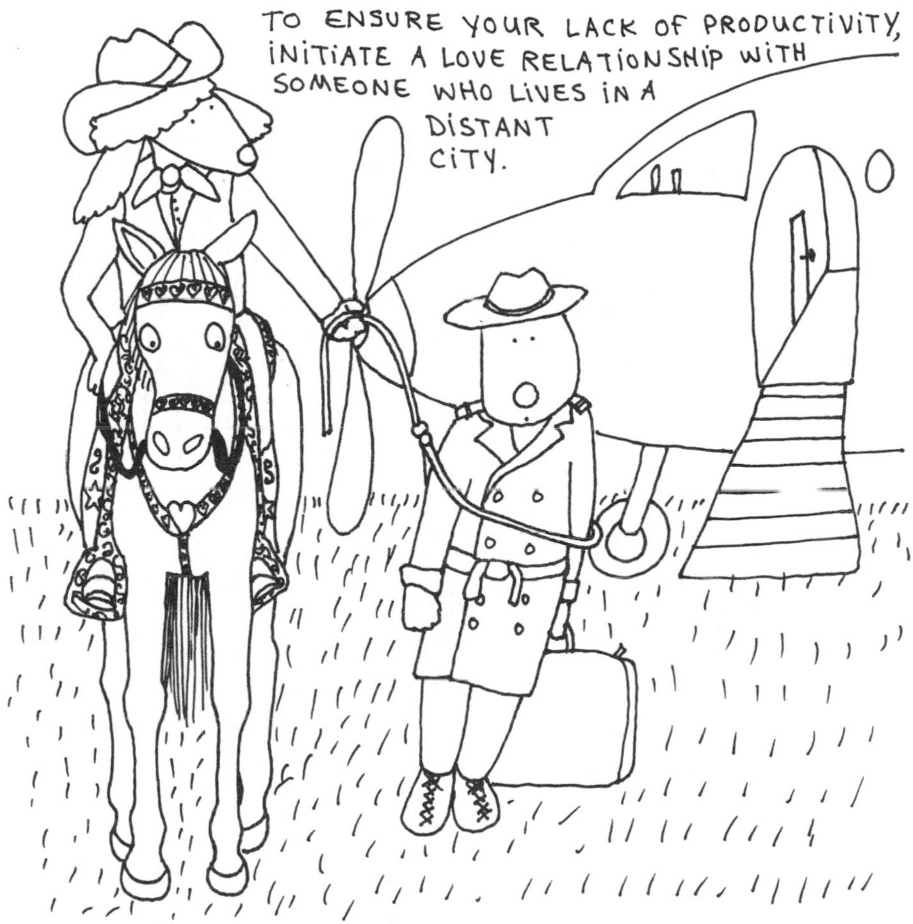
TO ENSURE YOUR LACK OF PRODUCTIVITY, INITIATE A LOVE RELATIONSHIP WITH SOMEONE WHO LIVES IN A DISTANT CITY.

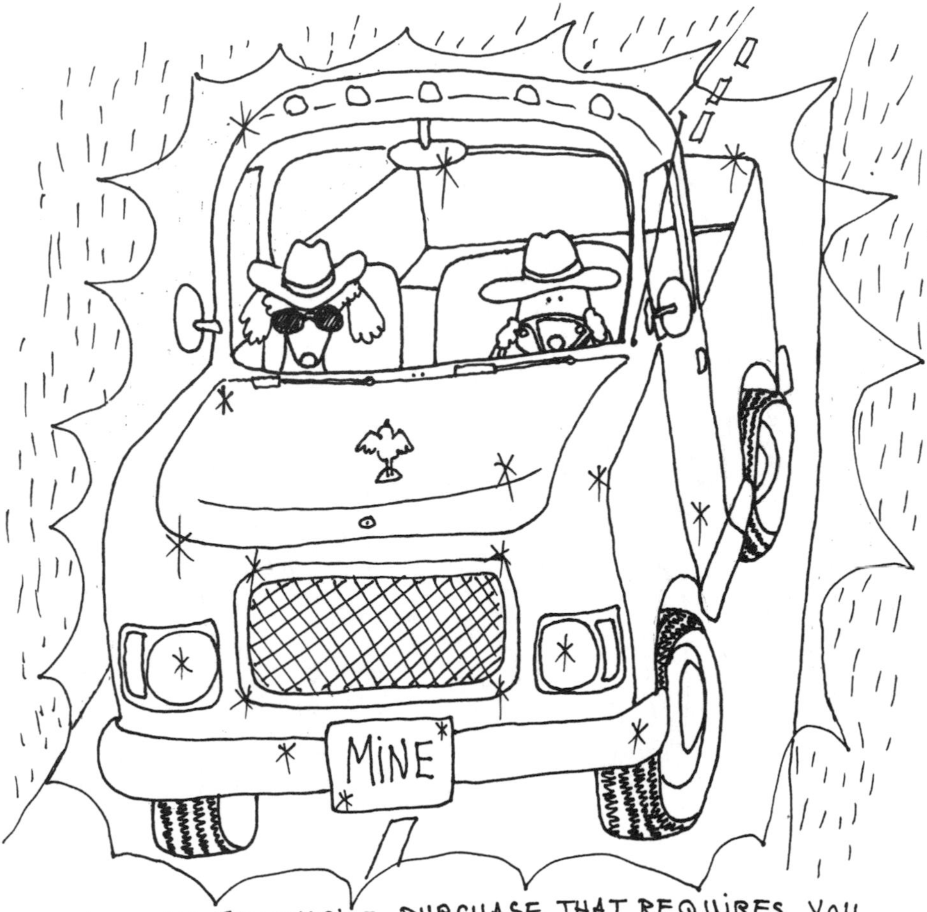
MiNE

MAKE AN EXPENSIVE PURCHASE THAT REQUIRES YOU TO WORK OVERTIME TO MAKE THE PAYMENTS.

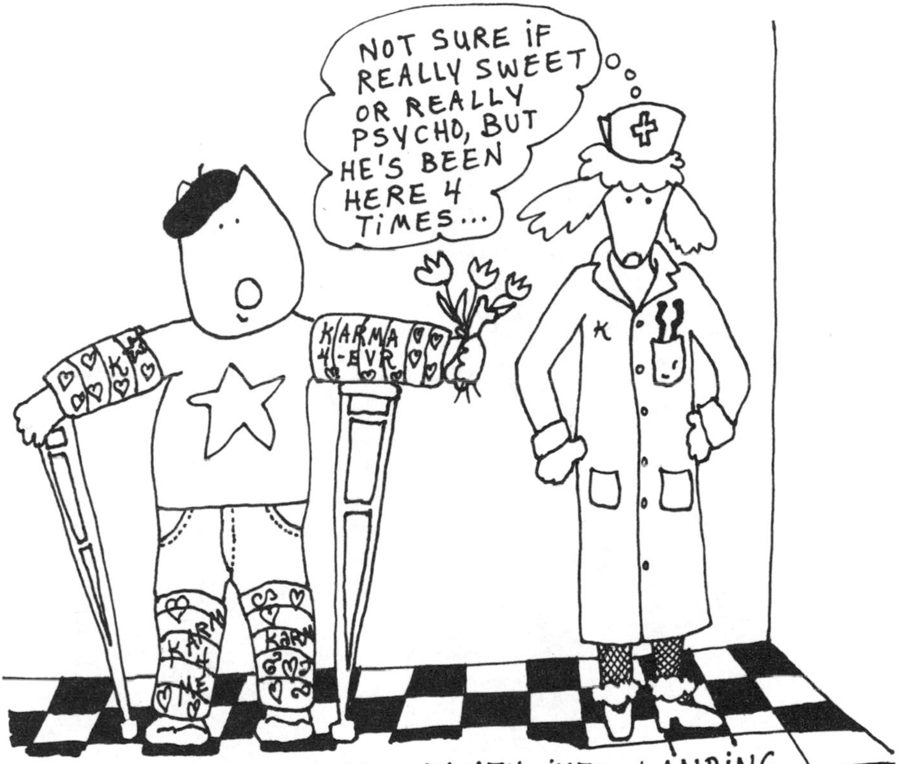
NOT SURE iF REALLY SWEET OR REALLY PSYCHO, BUT HE'S BEEN HERE 4 TiMES...
KARMA 4-EVR

FUNNEL ALL YOUR CREATiViTY iNTO LANDiNG AN ELUSiVE ROMANTiC QUARRY.

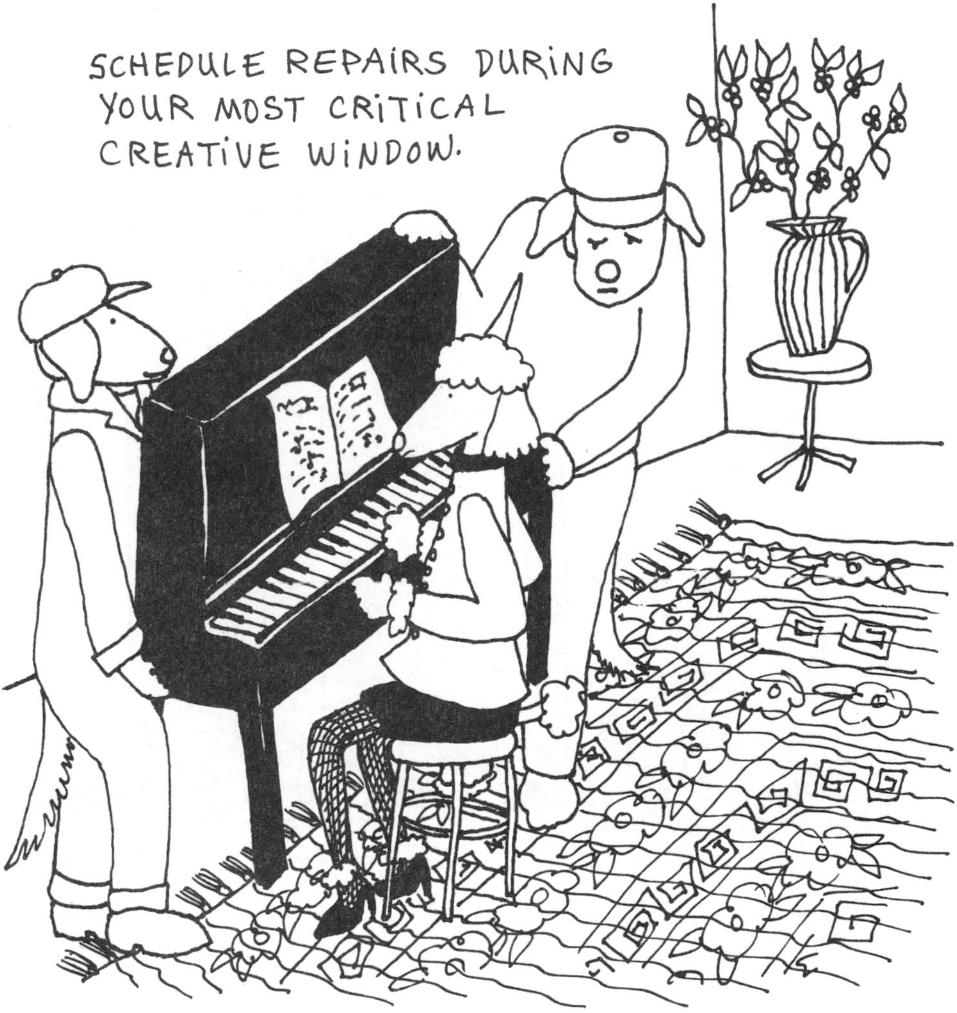

SCHEDULE REPAIRS DURING YOUR MOST CRITICAL CREATIVE WINDOW.

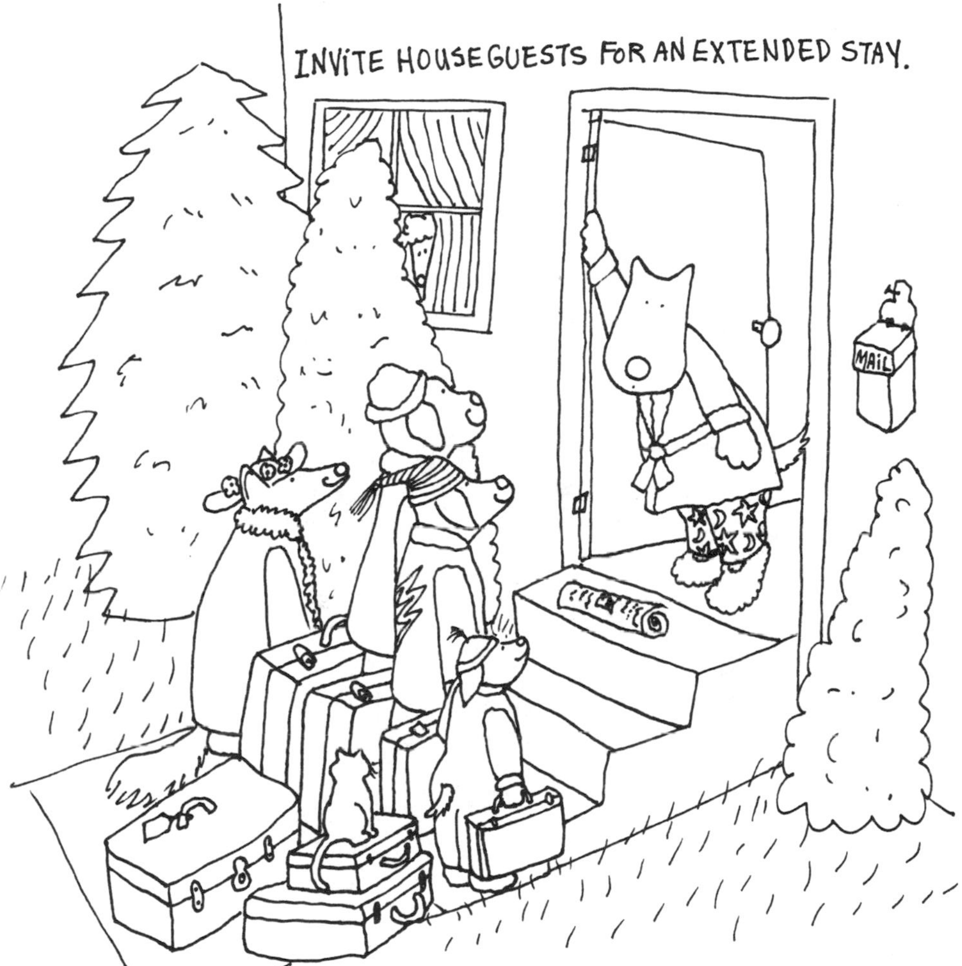
MAIL

INVITE HOUSEGUESTS FOR AN EXTENDED STAY.

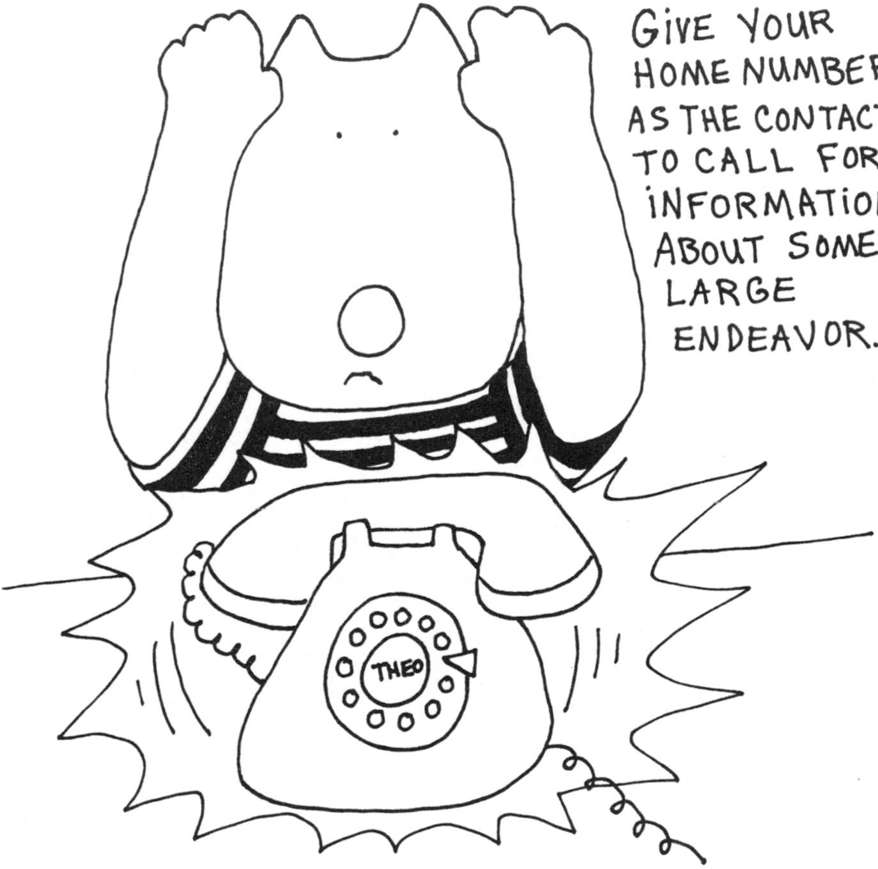
THEO

GIVE YOUR HOME NUMBER AS THE CONTACT TO CALL FOR INFORMATION ABOUT SOME LARGE ENDEAVOR.

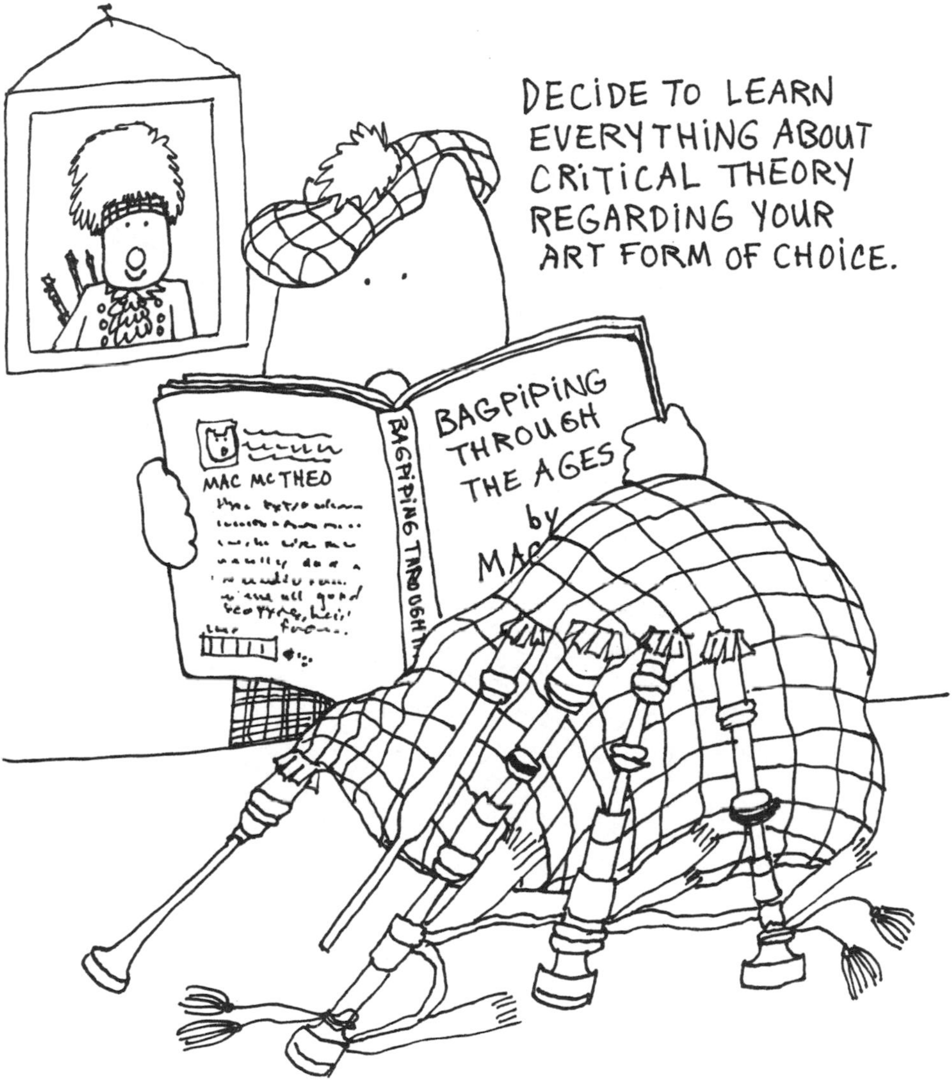
DECIDE TO LEARN EVERYTHING ABOUT CRITICAL THEORY REGARDING YOUR ART FORM OF CHOICE.
BAGPIPING THROUGH THE AGES by MAC
BAGPIPING THROUGH
MAC MCTHED

TELL YOURSELF YOU'LL FEEL MORE LIKE DOING ART AFTER YOU CHECK YOUR STOCKS AGAIN.

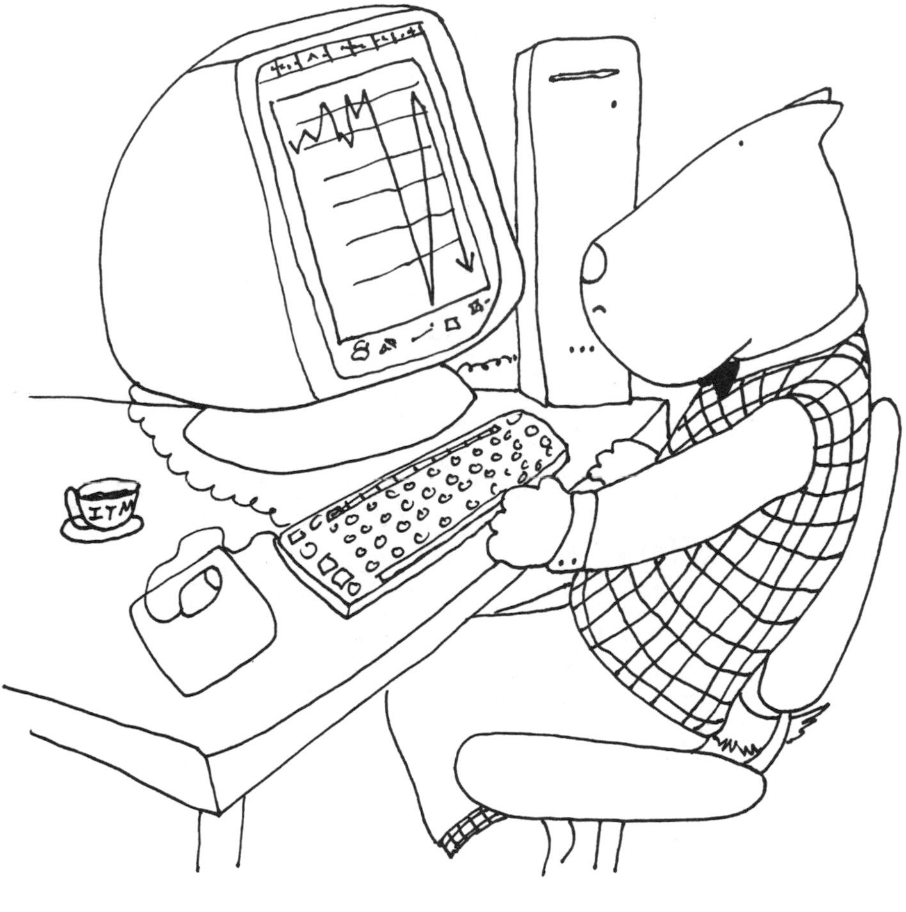
ITM

SPEND AN EXCESSIVE AMOUNT OF QUALITY
TIME WITH YOUR SIGNIFICANT OTHER. THEN
SPEND MORE.

RATHER THAN WRITE YOUR NOVEL, TYPE YOUR SIGNIFICANT OTHER'S THESIS.

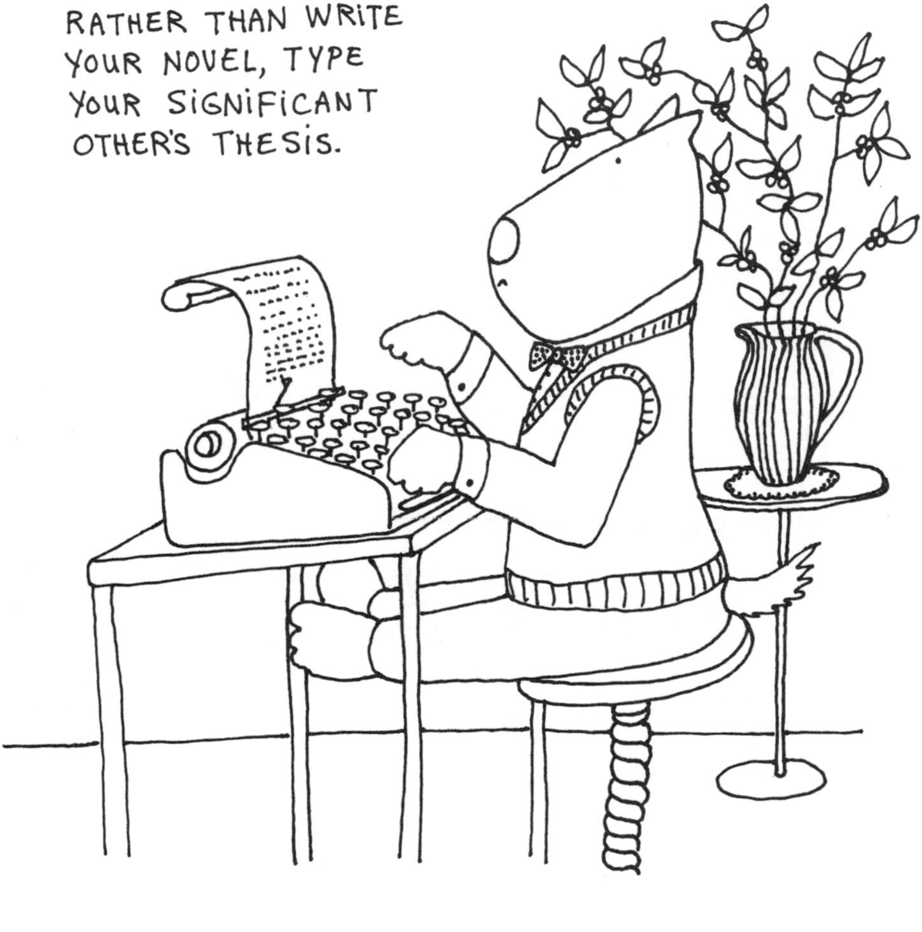

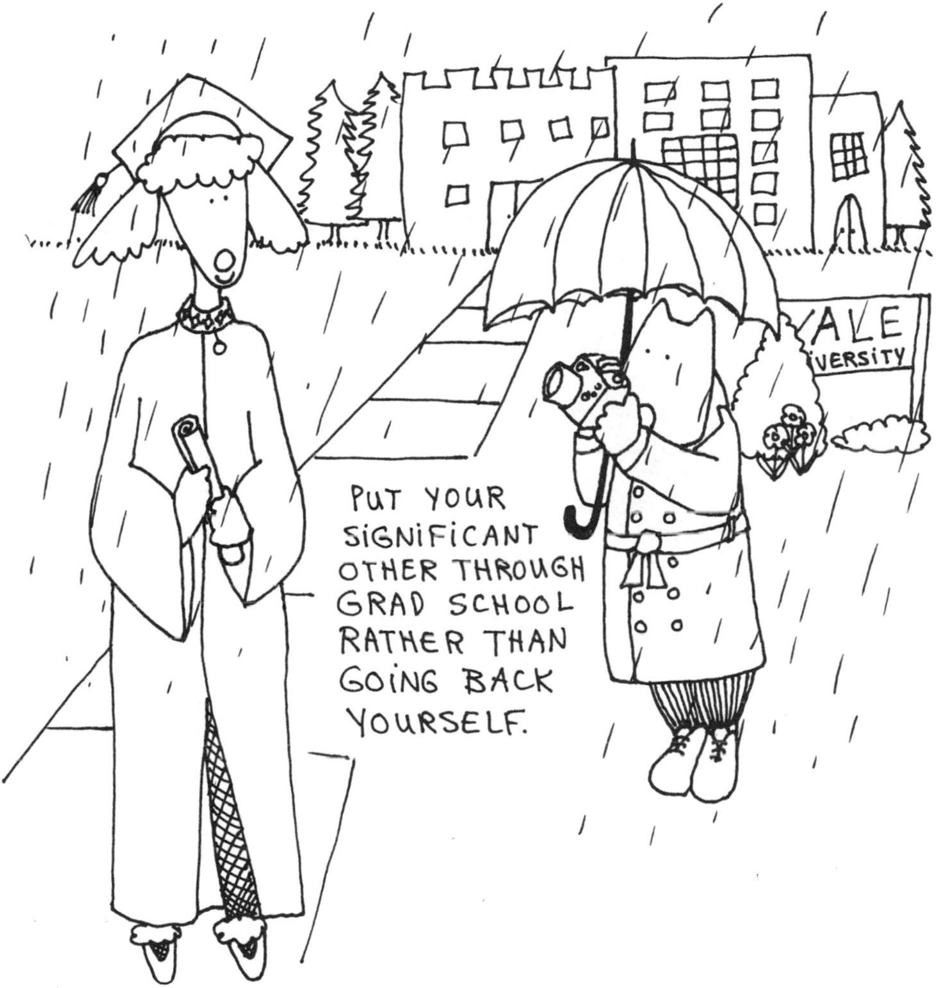
ALE
VERSITY
PUT YOUR SIGNIFICANT OTHER THROUGH GRAD SCHOOL RATHER THAN GOING BACK YOURSELF.

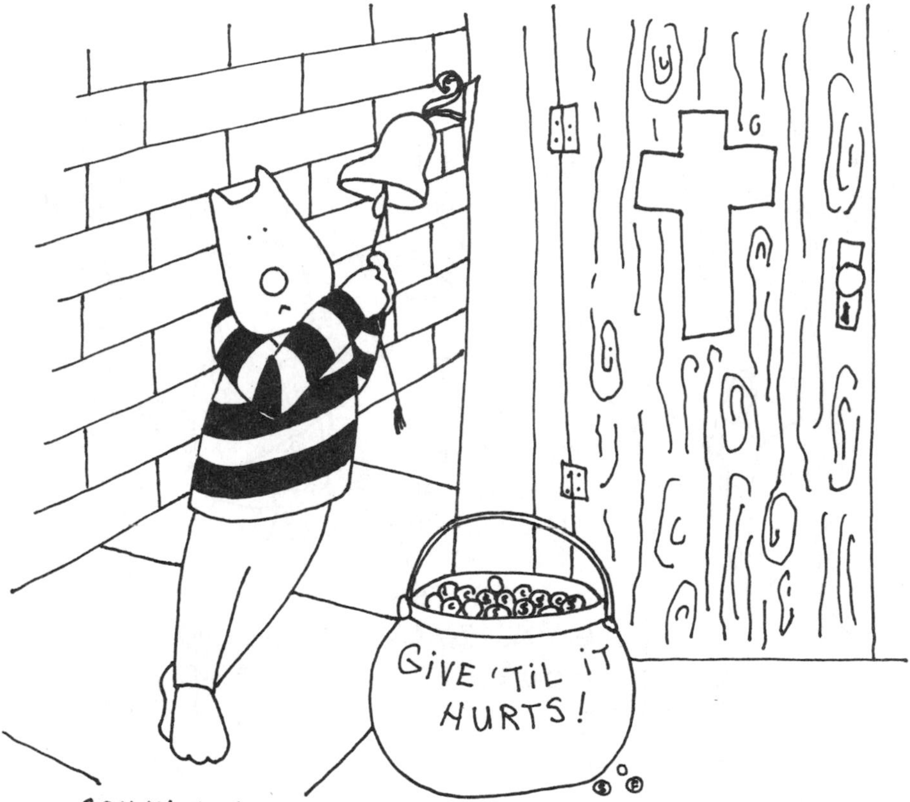
GIVE 'TIL IT HURTS!

COMMIT YOURSELF TO AN UNSPECIFIED NUMBER OF HOURS ON A COMMUNITY PROJECT.

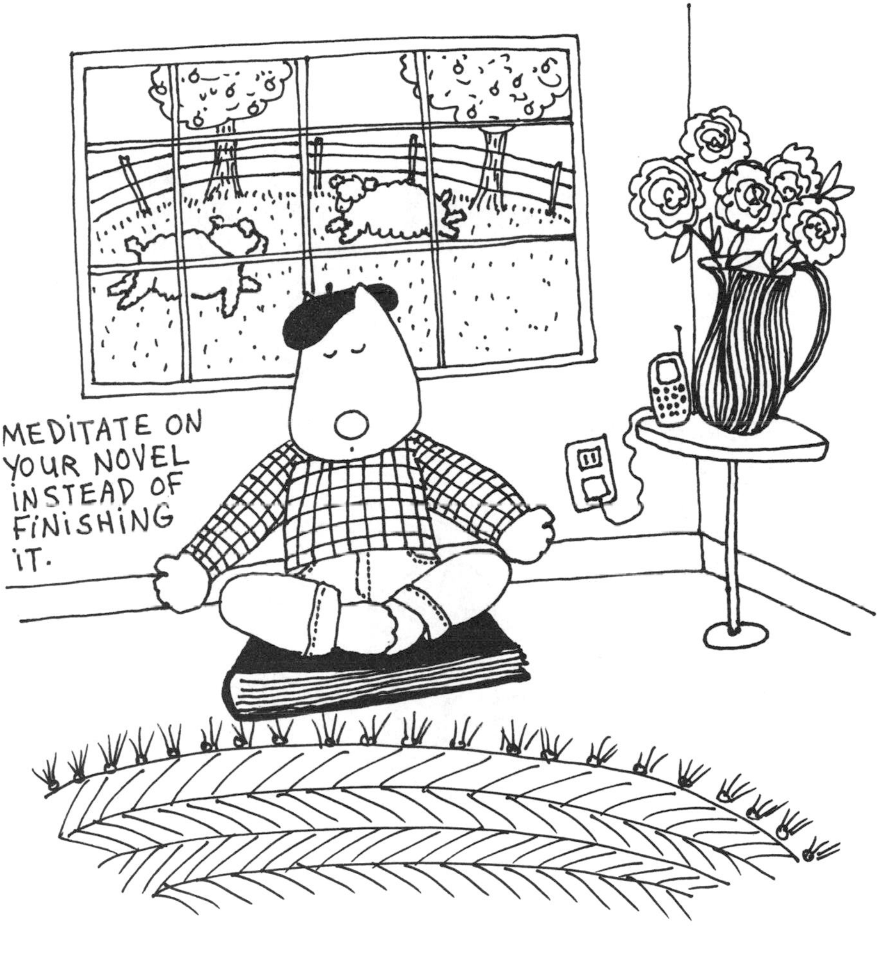
MEDITATE ON YOUR NOVEL INSTEAD OF FINISHING IT.

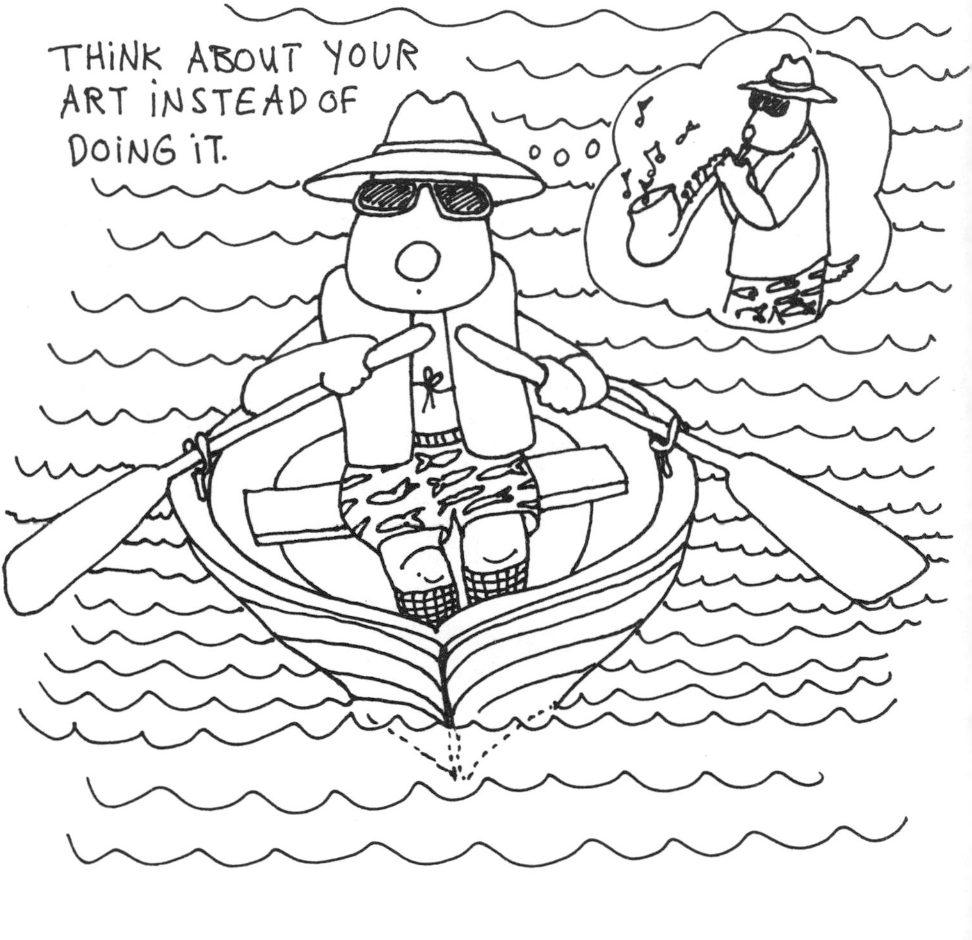
THINK ABOUT YOUR ART INSTEAD OF DOING IT.

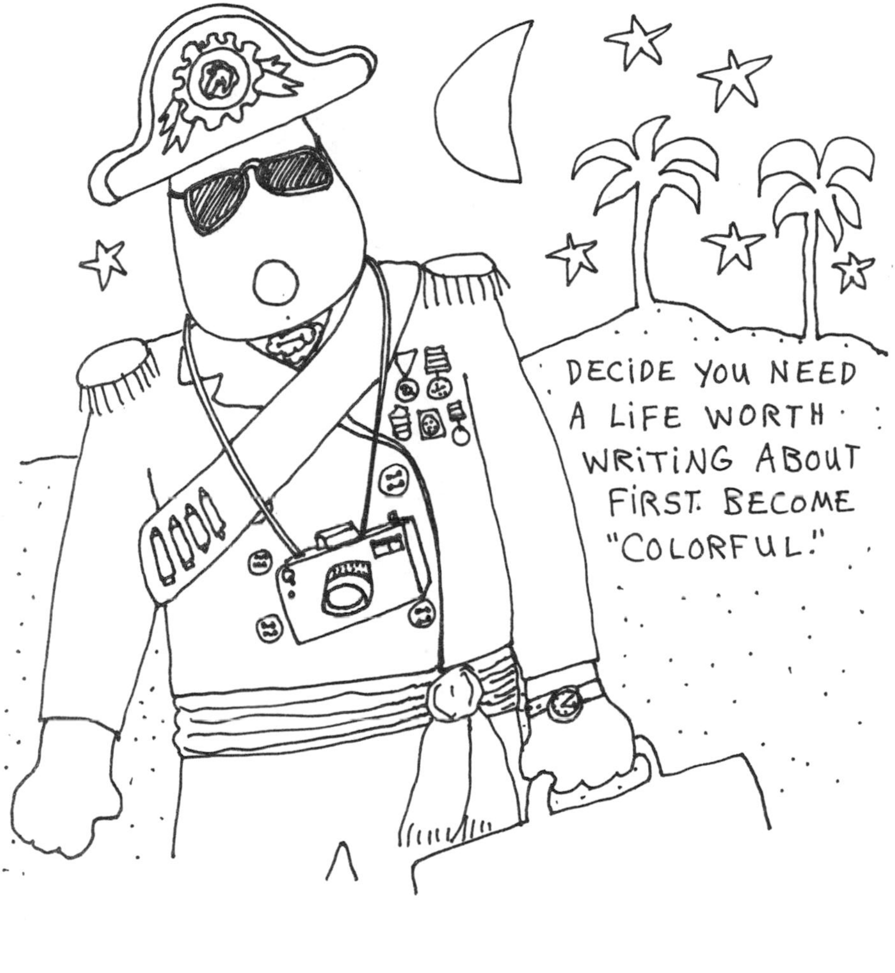
DECIDE YOU NEED A LIFE WORTH WRITING ABOUT FIRST. BECOME "COLORFUL."

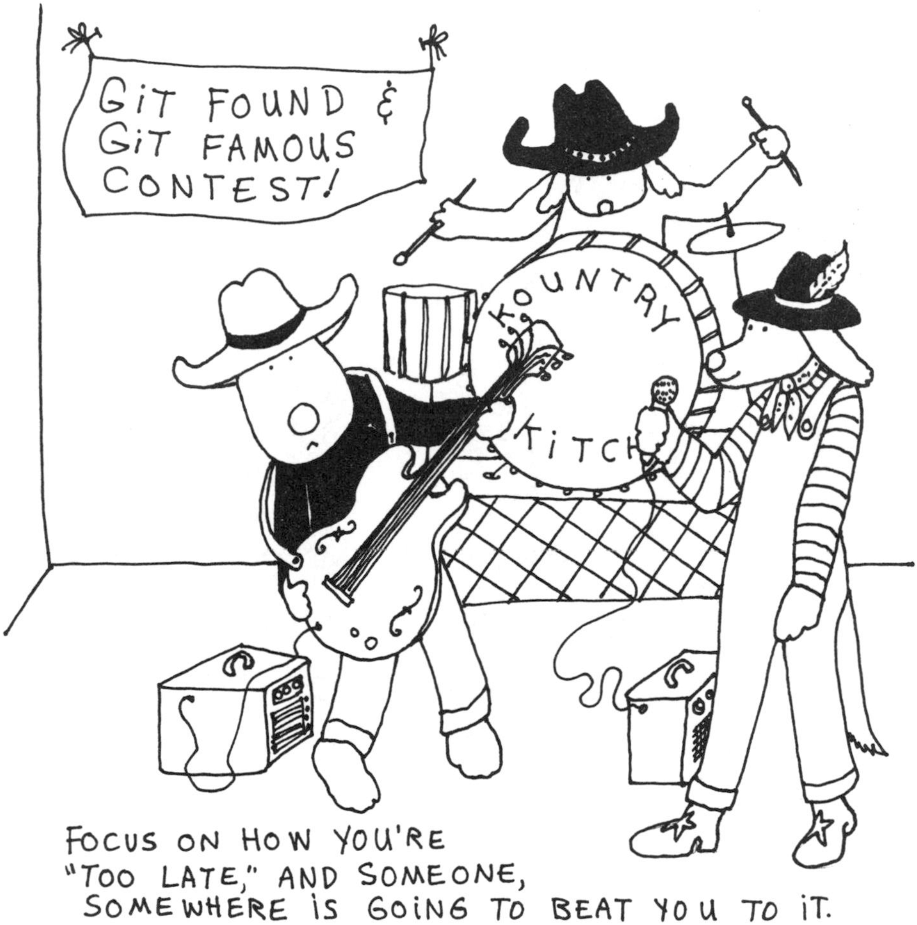
GiT FOUND &
GiT FAMOUS
CONTEST!
KOUNTRY
KiTCH

FOCUS ON HOW YOU'RE "TOO LATE," AND SOMEONE, SOMEWHERE IS GOING TO BEAT YOU TO IT.

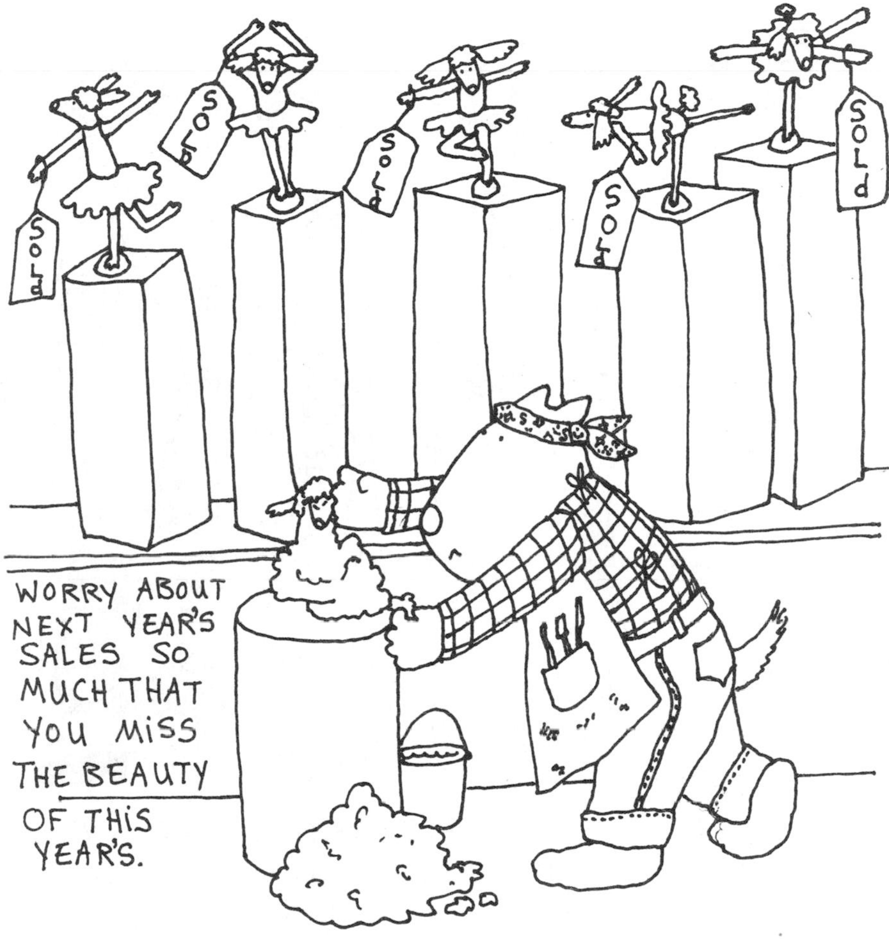
SOLd
SOLd
SOLd
SOLd
SOLd
WORRY ABOUT NEXT YEAR'S SALES SO MUCH THAT YOU MISS THE BEAUTY OF THIS YEAR'S.

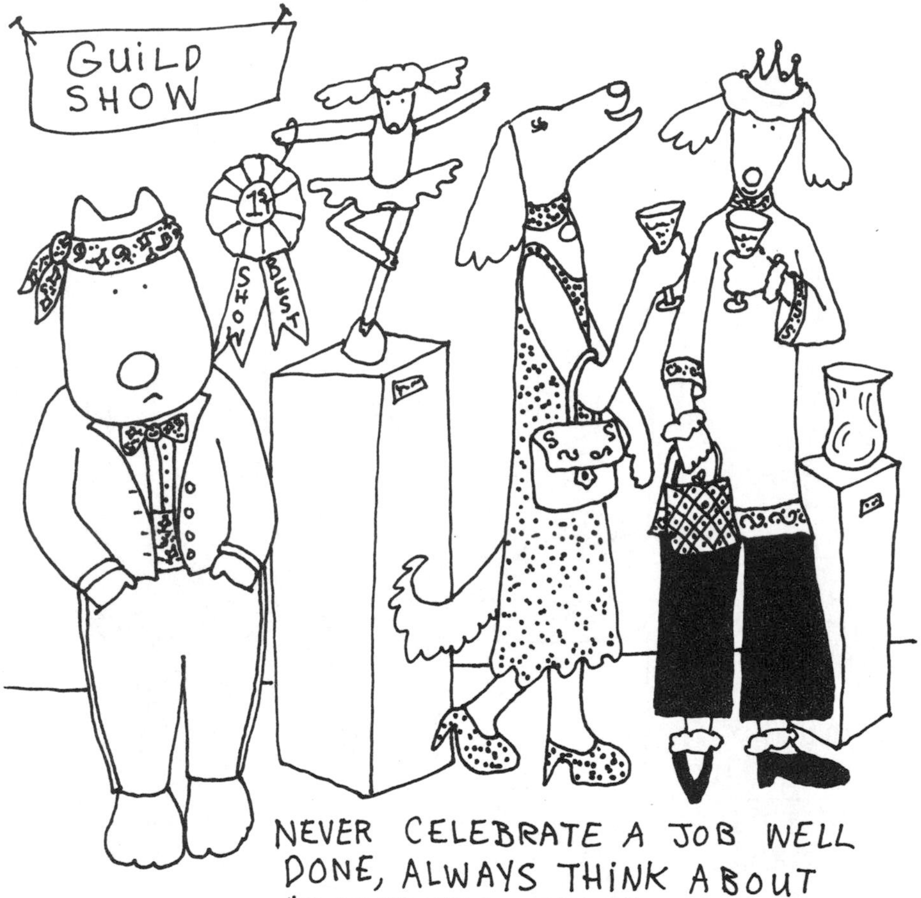
GUILD SHOW
1st
BEST
SHOW

NEVER CELEBRATE A JOB WELL DONE, ALWAYS THINK ABOUT "MORE" THAT NEEDS DOING.

CULTIVATE A NEGATIVE AND TIME CONSUMING PERSON. MAKE THEM YOUR BEST FRIEND.

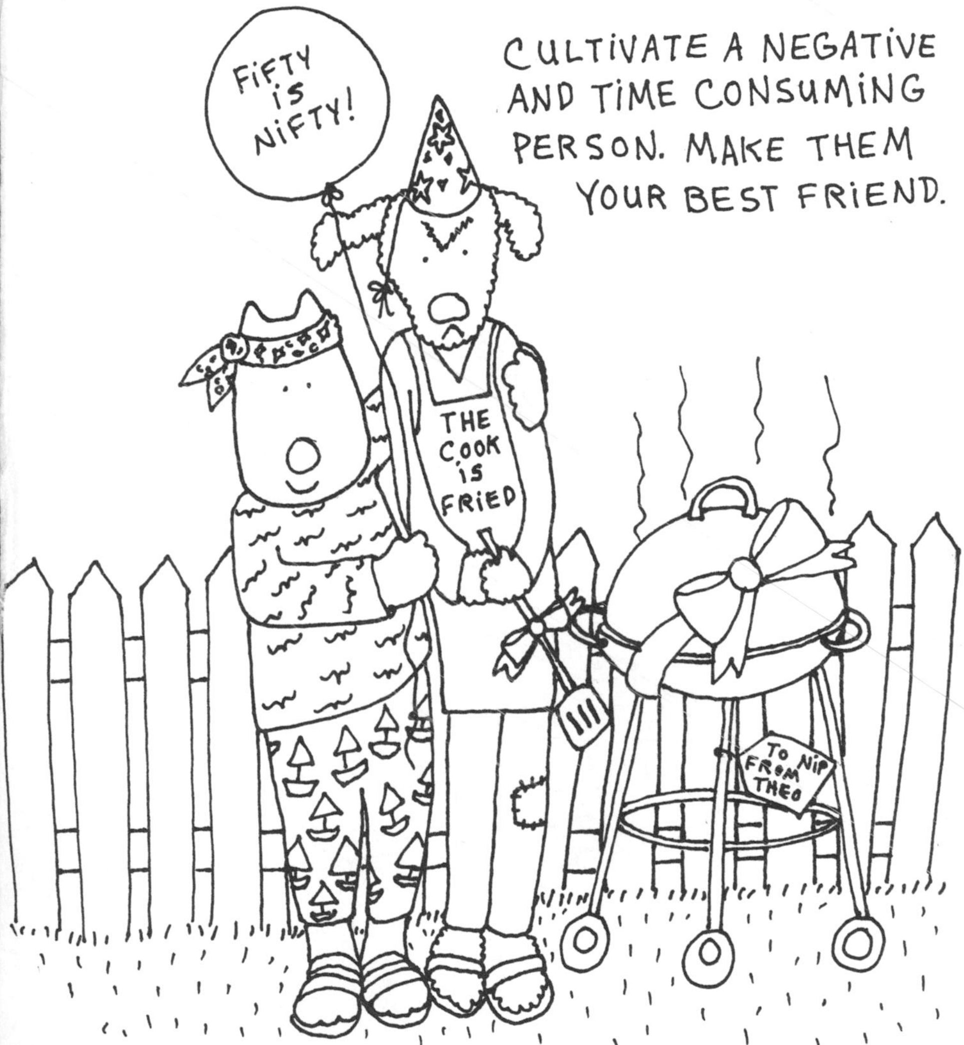
FIFTY IS NIFTY!
THE COOK IS FRIED
TO NIP FROM THEO

TO ENSURE
YOUR LACK OF
PRODUCTIVITY,
PRACTICE YOUR
ART IN THE
MOST DIFFICULT
AND UNCOMFORTABLE
WAY POSSIBLE.
TELL YOURSELF
IT IS DISCIPLINE.

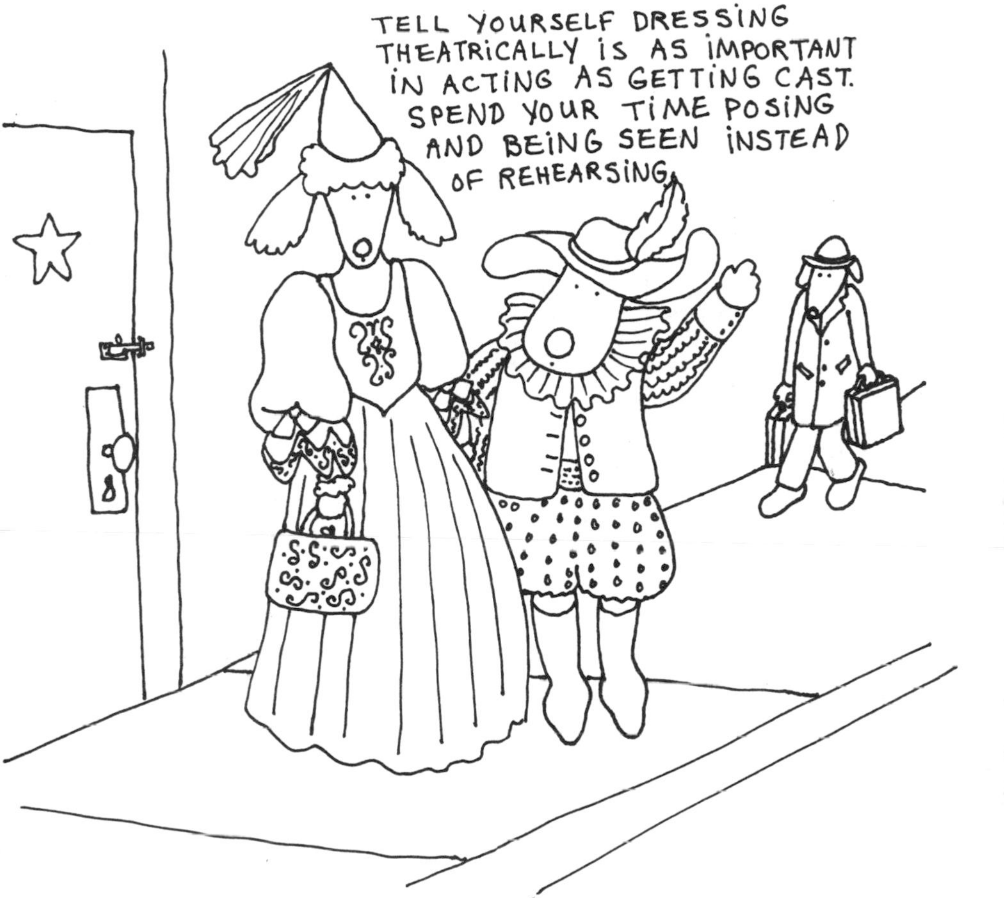
TELL YOURSELF DRESSING THEATRICALLY IS AS IMPORTANT IN ACTING AS GETTING CAST. SPEND YOUR TIME POSING AND BEING SEEN INSTEAD OF REHEARSING.

WASTE YOUR TIME FALLING FOR A GARDEN VARIETY CHEAT.
BECOME A TROPHY SPOUSE. SPEND YOUR LIFE TRYING TO
PLEASE INSTEAD OF CREATING A
VIABLE CAREER WITH YOUR ART.

HiDE FROM THE
CRAZYMAKERS
iN YOUR LiFE
iNSTEAD OF
SETTiNG
BOUNDARiES.
HiDiNG MAKES
iT HARD TO DO
YOUR ART.

About the Author

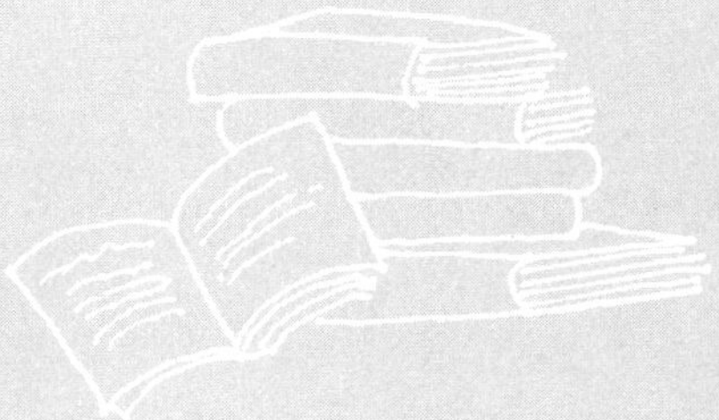

Julia Cameron has been an active artist for more than thirty years. She is the author of nineteen books, both fiction and nonfiction, including her bestselling works on the creative process: *The Artist's Way*, *Walking in This World*, *The Vein of Gold*, *The Right to Write*, and *The Sound of Paper*. A novelist, playwright, songwriter, and poet, she has multiple credits in theater, film, and television.